MW01231290

4U

Mormon Beliefs

and What the Bible Says

GABRIEL HUGHES

WWUTT.com

ISBN 978-1793029751

Second Edition

For best results, read with your Bible open.

Table of Contents

Introduction

Mormonism is the religious tradition of the Church of Jesus Christ of Latter-day Saints. The religion gets its name from the Book of Mormon, a sacred text said to have been written by the hand of Mormon and translated by Joseph Smith. It was first printed in 1830.

Joseph Smith is the founder of the Mormon faith and considered to be their greatest prophet, to whom God revealed himself and his word. In addition to the Book of Mormon, the canon of works that the Mormons consider sacred include the Holy Bible (King James Version), Pearl of Great Price, and Doctrine and Covenants.

Mormonism was born during what was called the Restoration Movement that came out of the Second Great Awakening. Restorationism is the idea that Christianity needs to be restored to the tenets of the early apostolic church of the first century. Joseph Smith taught that the denominations of his day were a corruption of the church, and that the Church of Jesus Christ of Latter-day Saints was a God-ordained return to the true apostolic tradition.

This book will present forty Mormon beliefs, divided into five chapters with eight points each, and what the Bible says regarding each belief. Because the translation of the Bible most accepted by the Mormon church is the King James Version, many passages are presented in the KJV. Others are given in the English Standard Version for easier reading and clarification.

Sources are cited, almost all of which are from Mormon publications, authors, apostles, and presidents, with only a few exceptions. I have tried to present Mormon beliefs in their own words, fairly and accurately. May this serve as a helpful guide not only to understand Mormonism, but what the Bible teaches.

Because all of Mormonism hinges on what Joseph Smith claimed and taught, we will first examine what the Mormons believe about their prophet. Next, we'll see what the Mormon scriptures and teachers have said about God, Jesus Christ, attaining salvation, and right living.

The Bible says to test everything and hold fast to what is good (1 Thessalonians 5:21). May we learn how to test all things according to the word of God!

Pastor Gabriel Hughes

A brief Biography of Joseph Smith

Joseph Smith Jr. was born in Vermont on December 23, 1805, the fifth of eleven children. His father, Joseph Sr., was a farmer and a Freemason who believed in the Christian God, but he did not care for organized religion and would not take his family to church. He said "that there was no order or class of religionists that knew anymore concerning the kingdom of God" than those who "made no profession of religion whatever."[1]

Old Joe, as he was known, claimed to receive spiritual guidance through dreams and visions from God. These dreams of his were mostly about his disgust with the Protestant denominations and how God was going to raise up something better. He left the religious upbringing of his children to their mother, Lucy Mack Smith.

Lucy came from a family that believed spiritual experiences trumped tradition and doctrinal fidelity, rebelling against the puritan theology of Jonathan Edwards and George Whitefield preached throughout New England. Following that time of theological revival known as the Great Awakening, restorationism started sweeping the American northeast. Restorationists, also known as Seekers, "anticipated a

---

[1] Peterson, Scott R., *Where Have All the Prophets Gone?* (Cedar Fort, Springville, UT; 2005). Pg. 348.

restoration or some kind of authority to administer the church and its ordinances of salvation."[2]

One of the more accomplished Seekers was Lucy's brother, Jason Mack, who amassed a significant following. Like many Seekers, Jason claimed to be able to heal the sick and receive special revelation from God. He believed "there was no church in existence which held to the pure principles of the gospel,"[2] but that through prayer God would eventually restore the blessings and privileges once enjoyed by the early disciples of Jesus.

Jason and Lucy's father, Solomon, was given to wild and fanciful visions also. Solomon came from a long line of clergy, but he was unable to afford seminary. Largely unschooled, he still managed to write a book of his religious experiences. Joseph Jr. grew up listening to this book read aloud to him and his siblings by his mother.

In 1817, after three years of crop failures and a bad business deal, Joseph Sr. moved the family to western New York. A lot of movement and migration was going through the area in those days, bringing restless attitudes of discontentment and nonconformity, especially in the church. Many denominations experienced schisms, most notably the Methodists, Baptists, and Presbyterians. All of these

---

[2] Givens, Tarryl L., *Wrestling the Angel: The Foundations of Mormon Thought: Cosmos, God, Humanity* (Oxford University Press, 2015). Pg. 25.

things no doubt had a profound influence on the younger Joseph.

At the age of 25, Joseph Jr. published the Book of Mormon, an additional testament of Jesus Christ which Smith claimed he received from an ancient text given to him by an angel on gold plates. The book is presented as a historical account of three main peoples in ancient America—the Jaredites, Nephites, and Lamanites.

The Jaredites came to America after the Tower of Babel in Genesis 11. The Nephites and Lamanites are descendants of Lehi who left Jerusalem and came to America at the time of the Babylonian exile of the Jews (around 600 B.C.). Most of the book is about the conflicts between these latter two groups. The story culminates with the appearance of Christ, who came from heaven to America after his resurrection to preach the gospel to the Native Americans.

After publication, Smith immediately planted his first church. He spoke of supernatural signs and wonders, heavenly visions, prophetic divination, higher knowledge, new baptism, and personal encounters with biblical figures. He also presented witnesses to these revelations, like Oliver Cowdery, who wrote the Book of Mormon as Smith dictated.[3]

---

[3] David Whitmer, one of the Three Witnesses, gave a detailed recollection of how Smith and Cowdery wrote the Book of Mormon in an interview with the *Kansas City Journal* in June, 1881. http://www.whitmercollege.com/published/interviews/kansas -city-journal-1881

During the restoration movement, many people longed for a more experiential form of worship. Kindled by religious fervor, Pentecostalism spread like fire with groups claiming to speak in tongues, experience miraculous healing, roll on the ground in spiritual ecstasy, and receive new revelation from God. It was the perfect environment for Smith to find adherents for his new religion.

However, western New Yorkers were skeptical of Smith. He was known among the locals as a treasure-seeker and a con-man. One of his cons had involved a wealthy farmer in Chenango County whom Smith convinced he could find buried treasure by looking through a certain seer stone. New York had strict laws against "pretending to tell fortunes, or to discover where lost goods may be found," and he was taken to court for disorderly conduct.[4]

Opposition against him grew quickly, and in the same year Smith started churches in New York, he fled for Ohio and Missouri where churches planted by other Mormon leaders were thriving. Mormonism found willing audiences among other seekers. A few hundred converts turned into tens of thousands in less than a decade. Several Mormon settlements and communities were founded and new temples were erected. By 1833, Smith gave his church the name

---

[4] An assessment of those proceedings can be found at this website: https://web.archive.org/web/20110609204410/http://mormonscripturestudies.com/ch/dv/1826.asp

Church of Latter-day Saints, and after a revelation in 1838, he officially changed it to the Church of Jesus Christ of Latter-day Saints.

The theocratic religion brought Joseph Smith much acclaim, revered by his most loyal followers as a prophet of God. But outside Mormonism, many saw the church as a cult and nothing but trouble. When antagonists came against the Mormons, Smith first encouraged his followers to peacefully endure, but later he adopted a more militant response. Non-Mormons forced Mormons from their homes, and Mormons retaliated by expelling the unconverted from their homes. This led to the 1838 Mormon War in northwest Missouri and a lesser-known conflict in Illinois. Smith was also charged with treason and spent time in jail.

In addition to provoking outside conflict, Smith caused turmoil within Mormonism itself. Not every-one agreed with Smith's political ambitions. Even longstanding leaders were expelled for expressing disapproval, including Oliver Cowdery (he would be rebaptized into the church after Smith's death). Still, the religion continued to advance with new converts in Europe through a mission led by Brigham Young, president of the Quorum of Twelve Apostles. Many wealthy investors joined the religion. A new settle-ment was founded in Iowa, and a town in Illinois called Nauvoo.

During the Nauvoo years, Smith introduced new

doctrines into church canon, including baptism of the dead, belief in many gods, and plural marriage. Smith had several dozen wives, by some accounts; ten of whom were already married to other men. Some willingly gave their wives to Smith, but others did not consent. The eventual riot that led to Smith's death was partly motivated by the anger of jealous husbands.

In his last days, Joseph Smith was a mayor, and even declared his candidacy for president of the United States. He possessed his own militia and secret police force; he threatened or excommunicated anyone who disagreed with him; he was accused of using polygamy to seduce women; he approved burning down a newspaper that had published a single issue to warn people about Mormonism; and he declared martial law to prevent further uprisings.

The governor of Illinois ordered Smith and the city council of Nauvoo to turn themselves in or be taken by force. Smith initially tried to flee, but the state of Missouri was also after him for treason. Instead Smith and his brother Hyrum surrendered and were put in jail in Carthage, IL, along with two other men.

Just days after being arrested, an armed mob stormed the jail. Joseph and Hyrum both had guns which had been smuggled in for them by sympathizers. They discharged all their rounds but were powerless to fight back. Hyrum was killed by a shot to the face and Joseph was struck in the back, sending him careening out a second-story window. A witness heard him shout "Oh Lord, my God!" as he fell. Upon hitting the ground, the awaiting militia gunned Smith down and killed him.

On June 27, 1844, Joseph Smith was declared dead of multiple gunshot wounds. He was 38 years old and regarded as a martyr by his followers. When his body was returned in a coffin to Nauvoo, twenty thousand Mormons came to pay their respects. His body is there in Nauvoo to this day.

After Smith's death, Brigham Young assumed leadership and led an exodus of 1,600 Mormons out of Nauvoo to escape persecution. In the fall of 1846, they settled in the Valley of the Great Salt Lake in the Utah territory. By the time Young died in 1877, the valley was populated with nearly 100,000 Mormons.

Today Mormonism has an estimated 16 million adherents worldwide, 60 percent of whom live outside the United States. The highest concentration of Mormons is still in the state of Utah. The Church of Jesus Christ of Latter-day saints has around 160 temples and over 30,000 local congregations (referred to in the LDS church as wards and branches).

More about the life of Joseph Smith and what he believed and taught will be expounded upon in the pages ahead.

What the Mormons Believe About
Joseph Smith

1) Joseph Smith is God's prophet.

The Mormons believe Joseph Smith (1805-1844) is a prophet of God. His being appointed as a prophet and the writing of the Book of Mormon was prophesied in the Bible in Ezekiel 37:15-28. The stick of Judah and the stick of Joseph mentioned there describe the Bible and the Book of Mormon respectively, and the two will become one in God's hand. The "stick" is like a wooden rod around which ancient scrolls were wrapped.

The Book of Mormon, which came from Joseph Smith, prophesied about Smith in 2 Nephi 3. The preface to the chapter reads, "Joseph in Egypt saw the Nephites in a vision—He prophesied of Joseph Smith, the latter-day seer; of Moses, who would deliver Israel; and of the coming forth of the Book of Mormon. About 588-570 B.C."

What the Bible Says:

In the King James Bible, Ezekiel 37:16-17 reads like this: "Moreover, thou son of man, take thee one stick, and write upon it, For Judah, and for the children of Israel his companions: then take another stick, and write upon it, For Joseph, the stick of Ephraim and for all the house of Israel his companions: And join them one to another into one stick; and they shall become one in thine hand."

The "Joseph" in v.16 is clearly not Joseph Smith but Joseph the father of Ephraim (Genesis 46:20) from whom would come the tribe of Ephraim (Joshua 14:4). In Ezekiel 37, Ephraim represents the northern kingdom and Judah the southern kingdom, divided following Solomon's reign (the book of Hosea also refers to Israel, the northern kingdom, as Ephraim).

Ezekiel prophesied their rejoining. This had nothing to do with a Book of Mormon and the Bible. The word that appears in this passage for "stick" appears over a hundred times in the Old Testament, and it is always used to describe either a tree or wood (examples include Genesis 1:11, Exodus 31:5, Deuteronomy 28:36). Not one time is it used to describe a scroll. The picture then is more like two branches grafted together by God's hand.

The Bible says, "Long ago, at many times and in many ways, God spoke to our fathers by the prophets, but in these last days he has spoken to us by his Son" (Hebrews 1:1-2). We are told, "Beloved, do not believe every spirit, but test the spirits whether they are of God, for many false prophets have gone out into the world" (1 John 4:1). Joseph Smith's testimony is the utmost test of the Mormon faith. All of it is built on his teaching.

2) God the Father and God the Son appeared to Joseph Smith personally.

Joseph Smith claimed that at the age of 14, God the Father and God the Son appeared to him in a grove of trees near his parents' home in western New York. He wrote several accounts of what is called the First Vision, which have been the subject of much criticism as there are inconsistencies in his own recollections.

According to the most famous account written in the Pearl of Great Price, Smith had grown frustrated with the church, naming Presbyterians, Baptists, and Methodists in particular. Following the advice of James 1:5, he asked God for wisdom, and two persons of God appeared to him. One person said of the other, "This is my beloved son. Hear him!"

Smith asked which church he should join. God told him to join none of them for their professors were corrupt and their creeds were an abomination in his sight. God again forbade Smith to join any church, then disappeared.

What the Bible Says:

According to John 1:18, "No one has ever seen God; the only God, Jesus Christ, who is at the Father's side, has made him known." John also wrote, "No one has seen God at any time" (1 John 4:12). God told Moses in Exodus 33:20, "You cannot see my face, for no one may see me and live."[5] It is for this reason we can know Joseph Smith did not see God the Father.

If the Bible says no one can see God and no one has seen God, how are there various accounts of people in the Bible seeing God, such as Abraham, Jacob, and Isaiah? Because Abraham and Jacob both saw God in the appearance of a man, and who they saw was a pre-incarnate Christ, not the Father (Genesis 18:1-2, 32:24-30). What Isaiah saw was a vision, not the actual appearance of God, and whom he saw was a pre-incarnate vision of the Son (Isaiah 6:1-7). Again, no one has seen the Father.

Furthermore, Smith did not see the Son, either. In 1 Corinthians 15:5-8, the Apostle Paul gave a list of succession of those to whom Jesus appeared following his resurrection, including as many as five hundred brothers at one time (v.6). He said, "Last of all, as to one untimely born, he appeared also to me."

---

[5] Previously in verse 11, the Bible talks about God and Moses speaking face to face. But this is only a figure of speech to describe the closeness by which God and Moses spoke. Verse 20 clarifies Moses did not see God's face. See also Numbers 14:14.

Paul was the last to see Christ and be appointed as an apostle. Jesus' appearance to Paul was witnessed by the men who were with him (Acts 9:7) and his appointment as an apostle was verified by the other apostles (Acts 9:27, Galatians 2:9). There were no witnesses to Joseph Smith's claim that as a teenager he saw God.

No one will see Jesus again until his Second Coming, and it will be seen by the whole world. In Matthew 24:23-25, Jesus said, "Then if anyone says to you, 'Look, here is the Christ!' or 'There He is!' do not believe it. For false christs and false prophets will arise and perform great signs and wonders, so as to lead astray, if possible, even the elect. See, I have told you beforehand."

Joseph Smith did not see the Father nor the Son, nor has anyone else in this age who has claimed to have seen an appearance of God before their very eyes.

3) The Angel Moroni appeared to Joseph Smith and gave him the Book of Mormon.

The testimony of the prophet Joseph Smith is given at the beginning of the Book of Mormon. There it says that in 1823, again when Smith was still a teenager, the angel Moroni appeared to him with a message that God had a work for him to do. The two of them conversed all night through several appearances.

Moroni said that there was a book written on gold plates that gave an account of the former inhabitants of North America. With the plates were two seer stones in silver bows fastened to a breast-plate. Those stones, called Urim and Thummim, Smith would use to translate the writing on the plates. Moroni told Smith that the devil would try to tempt him to use the plates to get rich, but he must use the plates only for God's glory.

Smith found the location of the plates, but because he was under transgression, he couldn't take them with him. It was in the fourth year when he acquired the plates. Once the work of translation had concluded, Moroni took the plates back into his possession. They do not exist on earth today.

The Book of Mormon contains the names of eleven witnesses who are said to have seen the plates. The Three Witnesses claimed that an angel showed them the plates and they heard the voice of God. All three witnesses eventually broke fellowship with Smith and were excommunicated from the church. The other Eight Witnesses were all from either the Smith or Whitmer families, and said they were shown the plates by Smith rather than an angel.

In the introduction, the Book of Mormon states, "The Book of Mormon is a volume of holy scripture comparable to the Bible." According to Joseph Smith, it was "the most correct of any Book on earth and the keystone of our religion and a man would get nearer to God by abiding its precepts than by any other Book."[6]

The Mormons believe that over the centuries, the Bible became corrupted. According to the Articles of Faith, "We believe the Bible to be the word of God as far as it is translated correctly; we also believe the Book of Mormon to be the word of God."[7] So the Book of Mormon is the most correct book on earth, but the Bible has been corrupted and we need help to understand it rightly.

It was prophesied by Nephi in 600 B.C. that the words of the Bible would be changed: "For behold, they have taken away from the gospel of the Lamb many parts which are plan and most precious and also many covenants of the Lord have they taken away. And all this have they done that they might pervert the right ways of the Lord, that they might blind the eyes and harden the hearts of the children of men" (1 Nephi 13:26-27).[8]

It is through the Book of Mormon that the true church of Jesus Christ is realized, the Church of Jesus Christ of Latter-day Saints. All other churches are following false teaching.

---

[6] Wilford Woodruff journal, November 28, 1841, Church History Library, Salt Lake City.

[7] Article of Faith 8.

[8] This is a necessary position to maintain the Mormon faith. With so many contradictions between the Bible and the Book of Mormon, Mormonism is only able to hold that the Book of Mormon is true by claiming that the Bible is interpreted falsely.

What the Bible Says:

Galatians 1:8-9 reads, "But even if we *or an angel from heaven* should preach to you a gospel contrary to the one we preached to you, let him be accursed. As we have said before, so now I say again: If anyone is preaching to you a gospel contrary to the one you received, let him be accursed" (emphasis added).

Colossians 2:18 reads, "Let no one disqualify you, insisting on asceticism and worship of angels, going on in detail about visions, puffed up without reason by his sensuous mind." Jude 1:8 says, "In like manner these people also, relying on their dreams, defile the flesh, reject authority, and blaspheme the glorious ones."

Jesus said in Matthew 16:18 that he would build his church, and the gates of hell would not prevail against it. The idea that the former church failed and a new church was actualized through the Book of Mormon and the teaching of Joseph Smith would contradict Matthew 16:18 and insist that Jesus didn't know what he was talking about.

4) Joseph Smith translated the Book of Mormon from Reformed Egyptian.

It is believed that the plates given to Joseph Smith by the angel Moroni were written in a language called Reformed Egyptian. According to Moroni 9:32, "And now, behold, we have written this record according to our knowledge, in the characters which are called among us the reformed Egyptian, being handed down and altered by us according to our manner of speech." [9]

In the Pearl of Great Price, Joseph Smith claimed a copy of Reformed Egyptian characters was taken by Martin Harris to Charles Anthon, a professor at Columbia University. Anthon first claimed the translation was correct, and that the language was a mix of Egyptian, Chaldaic, Assyriac, and Arabic characters. He wrote a certificate authenticating the language, but upon finding out the book the characters originated from was given by an angel, he tore up the certificate (Joseph Smith—History 1:64-65).[10]

What the Bible Says:

In the book of Nehemiah, the Israelites had failed to keep the Law of God and had fallen into intermarrying with the pagan people God told them not

---

[9] There is no scholarship outside the Mormon religion that acknowledges the existence of such a language. All presentations of Reformed Egyptian characters have been determined to be frauds, including the Anthon Transcript.

[10] Upon hearing that his name was being used to authenticate Reformed Egyptian, Charles Anthon wrote a letter in to Eber D. Howe, editor of the *Painesville Telegraph* in Ohio. The letter was published in Howe's 1834 book *Mormonism Unvailed*. Anthon told him that the transcript he was presented with was a hoax containing characters from a hodgepodge of languages, inverted or turned on their sides, "anything else but 'Egyptian Hieroglyphics.'" He told Howe he had written him his full statement, "and must beg you, as a personal favor, to publish this letter immediately, should you find my name mentioned again by these wretched fanatics." (*Mormonism Unvailed*, pg 272).

to marry. We read in Nehemiah 13:23-27 just how shameful it was that half the children spoke a pagan language rather than the language of Judah. They were cursed and beaten and made to take an oath, reminded that Solomon fell into sin when he married foreign women who worshiped false gods. They were then cleansed of everything foreign (v.30), which would have included their language.

The point is this: the Book of Mormon would not have been written in such a pagan language as Reformed Egyptian by one of God's prophets at that point in history. Egypt was not heralded by Hebrews as a nation to be admired, nor was their language learned and cherished, regardless as to whether it was "altered." The Egyptians persecuted, enslaved, and killed the Hebrews. Before the common Greek, the words of the prophets were written in only two languages: Hebrew and Aramaic.

And—this might seem a minor technicality, but there's a point—Smith could not have *translated* the Book of Mormon from Reformed Egyptian into English. He did not know Reformed Egyptian, so he did no translating. By his own accounts, the seer stones allowed him to read Reformed Egyptian in English. Smith would have *transcribed* the Book of Mormon, making a copy in English of what he read in English.

Throughout the Book of Mormon, there are multiple ways Smith displayed a lack of understanding regarding languages.[11] For example, Alma, for whom the book of Alma is named, is a Hebrew name which means "Betrothed Virgin." It would not have been the name of a man. In 1 Nephi 2:5, Smith used the name Sam, an American name. Samuel is the Jewish name. In Jacob 7:27, Smith uses the word "Adieu," which is French, a language that did not exist in the 6th century B.C. when the book of Jacob was purportedly written.

These discrepancies are significant enough to reveal the faults of a man. They would not have been errors made by one of God's messengers and especially not God himself.

5) Through prayer, God will reveal that the Book of Mormon is true.

Moroni 10:4-5 reads, "And when ye shall receive these things, I would exhort you that ye would ask God, the Eternal Father, in the name of Christ, if these things are not true; and if ye shall ask with a sincere heart, with real intent, having faith in Christ, he will manifest the truth of it unto you, by the power of the Holy Ghost. And by the power of the Holy Ghost ye may know the truth of all things."

In the Pearl of Great Price, Joseph Smith mentioned that he prayed to God for wisdom according to James 1:5: "If any of you lack wisdom, let him ask

---

[11] Credit to Marian Bodine and the Creation Research Institute, Article ID: DM192, June 9, 2009.

of God, that giveth to all men liberally, and up-braideth not; and it shall be given him." He then claimed that God appeared to him and told him that all the churches were corrupt and an abomination to him.

This is why, if you've ever had a Mormon missionary come to your door, they invite you to pray and ask God to reveal to you that the Book of Mormon is true.

What the Bible Says:

Unlike the Book of Mormon, the Bible does not invite the reader to have a religious experience in order to verify its truthfulness. The Bible says the heart is wicked and not to be trusted. Jeremiah 17:9 says, "The heart is deceitful above all things, and desperately sick; who can understand it?" Proverbs 3:5 says to trust in the Lord and lean not on your own understanding. Proverbs 28:26 says whoever trusts in his own mind is a fool.

Religious experiences are subjective, not objective truth. We are to test all things not by our experiences but with the word of God. The Bereans tested the words of Paul against the Old Testament Scriptures to see if what he said was true (Acts 17:11).

Looking at the context of James 1:5, we read, "If any of you lacks wisdom, let him ask God, who gives generously to all without reproach, and it will be given him. But let him ask in faith, with no doubting, for the one who doubts is like a wave of the sea that is driven and tossed by the wind. For that person must not suppose that he will receive anything from the Lord; he is a double-minded man, unstable in all his ways."

Test Joseph Smith by those words: Did he not lack faith, expect something from God, was driven with the wind and tossed, and revealed to be double-minded and unstable in all his ways?

6) The Book of Mormon is another testament of Jesus Christ.

After 1981, printings of the Book of Mormon have featured on its cover the subtitle, "Another Testament of Jesus Christ." The purpose of the book as stated on its title page is to convince "the Jew and Gentile that Jesus is the Christ, the eternal God, manifesting himself unto all nations."

It's written in a mostly chronological order, detailing the events of the Jewish people in the Americas whose descendants became the Native American Indians. There are several appearances of Jesus hundreds of years before he was born in the Middle East.

Of central importance is his coming to the North American people, an event that happened shortly after his resurrection, but doesn't occur until 3 Nephi 11, almost at the end of the book. During his visit to the Americas, Jesus performed many miracles, healed the sick, taught his gospel, and called twelve disciples to build his church, as he had in Palestine.

Though Mormons claim that both the Bible and the Book of Mormon are the words of God, the Book of Mormon itself does not claim to be inspired by God. Rather, it claims over and over to be written according to the knowledge of men.

The book of 1 Nephi opens, "And I know that the record which I make is true; and I make it with mine own hand; and I make it according to my knowledge." In chapter 19, he said that he wrote down what he thought to be sacred (v.6). In 2 Nephi 11:1, he wrote down only that which "sufficeth me." And in Jacob 7:26, the writer said that he wrote to the best of his knowledge.

What the Bible Says:

In Galatians 1:6-7, Paul said, "I am astonished that you are so quickly deserting him who called you in the grace of Christ and are turning to a different gospel—not that there is another one, but there are some who trouble you and want to distort the gospel of Christ."

There is no other gospel. Yet the Book of Mormon has printed, right on the cover of the book, that it is "*Another* Testament of Jesus Christ."

Anyone who has read and understands the Bible would ask why it's necessary to have another testament of Jesus Christ. In the introduction of his letter,

Jude said that he was writing to contend for the faith "once for all delivered to the saints" (Jude 1:3). Proverbs 30:6 says not to add to the word of God, "lest he rebuke you and you be found a liar."

Again in Matthew 24:23-27, Jesus warned that if anyone says, "Look, here is the Christ!" or "There he is!" not to believe it. For false christs and false prophets would perform great signs and wonders so as to lead astray, if possible, even the elect. If someone says, "Look, he is in the wilderness," do not go out. If they say, "Look, he is in the inner rooms," do not believe it. For his next appearance will be seen by the whole world.

Unlike the Book of Mormon, the Bible does not claim to be the knowledge of man but was inspired by God. Paul wrote in 2 Timothy 3:16-17, "All Scripture is breathed out by God and profitable for teaching, for reproof, for correction, and for training in righteousness, that the man of God may be complete, equipped for every good work."

As it says in 1 Corinthians 2:13, "We impart this in words not taught by human wisdom but taught by the Spirit, interpreting spiritual truths to those who are spiritual." And 2 Peter 1:20-21 says, "No prophecy of Scripture comes from someone's own interpretation. For no prophecy was ever produced by the will of man, but men spoke from God as they were carried along by the Holy Spirit." Peter also said that he and the other apostles did not follow cleverly devised myths but were eyewitnesses to the majesty of God (2 Peter 1:16).

No historian has ever authenticated any of the events contained in the Book of Mormon. None of the North American cities mentioned in its pages have been discovered. None of their currency has been unearthed. There are no ancient writings from other people groups mentioning the peoples who are the focus of the Book of Mormon. There is no archaeological evidence at all. Its claims are unverifiable. To borrow Peter's phrasing, it is a cleverly devised myth. The Book of Mormon is, at best, historical fiction.

7) Joseph Smith taught he would become a god and take the place of God.

Joseph Smith said, "When I get my kingdom, I shall present it to my Father, so that he may obtain kingdom upon kingdom, and it will exalt him in glory. He will then take a higher exaltation, and I will take his place, and thereby become exalted myself."[12]

Boasting in himself, he preached, "I have more to boast of than ever any man had. I am the only man that has ever been able to keep a whole church together since the days of Adam. A large majority of the whole have stood by me. Neither Paul, John, Peter, nor Jesus ever did it. I boast that no man ever

---

[12] King Follett Discourse, 1844. Smith was talking about what Jesus saw his Father doing, and that Smith would do the same.

did such a work as I."[13]

Smith's successor, Brigham Young, said, "No man or woman in this dispensation will ever enter into the celestial kingdom of God without the consent of Joseph Smith… He reigns there as supreme being in his sphere, capacity, and calling as God does in heaven. Many will exclaim, 'Oh, that is very disagreeable! It is preposterous! We cannot bear the thought!' But it is true."[14]

What the Bible Says:

When Smith famously boasted of himself, he was preaching from 2 Corinthians 11. There the Apostle Paul was "boasting" about what he'd been through as an apostle. This was not to give Smith or any other a license to boast, for Paul called his own boasting folly and madness. Rather, he was trying to convince the Corinthians to turn away from false apostles, or whom he sarcastically called "chiefest apostles" (in some translations "super apostles") to whom he was not the least bit inferior (2 Corinthians 11:5).

By reading 2 Corinthians 11, it becomes clear that Joseph Smith did not accomplish more than the Apostle. Paul wrote, "Are they servants of Christ? I am a better one—I am talking like a madman—with far greater labors, far more imprisonments, with countless beatings, and often near death. Five times I

---

[13] History of the Church, Vol. 6, pg 408-409.
[14] Journal of Discourses, vol 7, pg 289-291.

received at the hands of the Jews the forty lashes less one. Three times I was beaten with rods. Once I was stoned. Three times I was shipwrecked; a night and a day I was adrift at sea" (v.23-25).

Paul went on to speak of his travels and perils, farther than Smith ever ventured or suffered. There is simply no comparison between the Apostle Paul and Joseph Smith. Paul said just as Eve was deceived in the garden, so the Corinthians were being deceived by false teachers.

"For such men are false apostles," Paul said, "deceitful workmen, disguising themselves as apostles of Christ. And no wonder, for even Satan disguises himself as an angel of light. So it is no surprise if his servants, also, disguise themselves as servants of righteousness" (v.13-15).

Paul was alerting the Corinthians to men who falsely claimed they were better apostles than he was. Isn't it ironic? The very passage Joseph Smith used to justify his boasting actually condemned his false teaching.

A man cannot ascend to become God. Isaiah 43:10 reads, "Before me there was no god formed, neither shall there be after me." And in Isaiah 45:5-6, "I am the Lord, and there is none else, there is no God beside me: I girded thee, though thou hast not known me: That they may know from the rising of the sun, and from the west, that there is none beside me. I am the Lord, and there is none else."

One might also recall God's response to Job: "Who is this that darkeneth counsel by words without knowledge?" (Job 38:2)

Though the Mormons believe Joseph Smith, like Paul, was martyred for his faith, aggression toward Smith was motivated by a variety of factors, including polygamy and polyandry, destroying a newspaper, perjury, treason, and inciting a riot — and that was just in his last few weeks. He had previously been charged with disorderly conduct in New York, escaped a charge of bank fraud in Ohio, narrowly avoided being hung in Missouri, and fled from custody to Illinois. Charges were brought against Smith by former associates and several state governments. Only he claimed his own innocence: "They pursue me without a cause" (Doctrine and Covenants, 127:1).

The Apostle Paul was executed by Rome for preaching Christ as Lord instead of Caesar. At his trials, no one could bring a single charge against him. Even the Roman officials said he would have been let go had he not appealed to Caesar (Acts 26:32).[15]

8) It is necessary to believe in Joseph Smith as God's prophet to attain salvation.

Doctrine and Covenants 135:3 says, "Joseph Smith, the Prophet and Seer of the Lord, has done

---

[15] Does Joseph Smith's claim to have done more than Christ really need any comment?

more, save Jesus only, for the salvation of men in this world, than any other man that ever lived in it." Joseph Fielding Smith, the tenth president of the LDS church, said that there is "no salvation without accepting Joseph Smith. If Joseph Smith was verily a prophet, and if he told the truth, no man can reject that testimony without incurring the most dreadful consequences, for he cannot enter the kingdom of God."[16]

Brigham Young said that whoever "does not confess that God has sent Joseph Smith, and revealed the everlasting gospel to and through him, is of Antichrist, no matter whether it is found in a pulpit or on a throne, nor how much divinity it may profess, nor what it professes with regard to revealed religion and the account that is given of the Savior and his Father in the Bible."[17]

To be sure that he didn't misspeak, Young said again, "He that confesseth not that Jesus has come in the flesh and sent Joseph Smith with the fullness of the gospel to this generation, is not of God, but is Antichrist."[18]

Referring to Young's teaching on Joseph Smith, former Mormon apostle George Q. Cannon said, "Joseph holds the keys." He added, "If we get our salvation, we shall have to pass by him; if we enter

---

[16] Doctrines of Salvation, vol. 1, pg 190.

[17] Journal of Discourses, vol 8, pg 176-177.

[18] Journal of Discourses, Vol 9, pg 312.

into our glory, it will be through the authority that he has received. We cannot get around him; we cannot get around President Young."

Regarding judgment, Cannon said, "Joseph, then, stands at the head; and then every man in his place after him," including the biblical apostles, who are behind Joseph Smith. "He will sit as a judge to judge those who have received or those who have rejected his testimony. He will stand as a swift witness before the judgment seat of God against this generation."[19]

In the Book of Mormon, 1 Nephi 21:8 reads, "Thus saith the Lord, In an acceptable time have I heard thee, O isles of the sea, and in a day of salvation have I helped thee; and I will preserve thee, and give thee my servant for a covenant of the people, to establish the earth, to cause to inherit the desolate heritages." The footnotes refer to 2 Nephi 3:11, which suggests that the servant for salvation is Joseph Smith.

What the Bible Says:

Isaiah 49:8 reads, "Thus saith the Lord, in an acceptable time have I heard thee, and in a day of salvation have I helped thee: and I will preserve thee, and give thee for a covenant of the people, to establish the earth, to cause to inherit the desolate heritages." Look familiar? That's because 1 Nephi 21:8 is quoting Isaiah 49:8 but adding in the words

---

[19] Journal of Discourses, Vol 23, pg 361.

"my servant" and then referring the reader to 2 Nephi 3:11 which mentions Joseph Smith.

This is the kind of slight-of-hand Smith would use to make it appear as if the Bible spoke of him. This is also the kind of thing that leads a Mormon to believe the Bible is the word of God "as far as it is translated correctly," while the Book of Mormon, Pearl of Great Price, and Doctrines and Covenants are perfect. Mormons judge the Bible based on the Mormon texts rather than judging the Mormon texts according to the Bible.

Deuteronomy 13:1-4 reads, "If a prophet or a dreamer of dreams arises among you and gives you a sign or a wonder, and the sign or wonder that he tells you comes to pass, and if he says, 'Let us go after other gods,' which you have not known, 'and let us serve them,' you shall not listen to the words of that prophet or that dreamer of dreams. For the Lord your God is testing you, to know whether you love the Lord your God with all your heart and with all your soul. You shall walk after the Lord your God and fear him and keep his commandments and obey his voice, and you shall serve him and hold fast to me."

The passage goes on to say that the prophet or dreamer of dreams shall be put to death. So it will be in judgment for any prophet who teaches falsely. Joseph Smith was not God's prophet. He taught people he would become a god and they would also become gods, which is the same as encouraging them to chase after other gods. The Scriptures are clear: men like Joseph Smith are liars.

Jesus said that his sheep hear his voice, he goes before them, and they follow him. His sheep will not follow the voice of a stranger but will flee from him. All who try to enter the sheepfold another way, except through Jesus Christ, are thieves and robbers. "The thief comes only to steal and kill and destroy. I came that they may have life and have it abundantly" (John 10:10).

Though Joseph Smith preached about God, it was a different god than the one of the Bible. Though Smith preached about Jesus Christ, it was a different Jesus than the one of the Bible. He spoke of salvation and right Christian living, but not according to what the Bible says. These are the things we will consider in the coming chapters.

What the Mormons Believe About
God

1) The first verse of the Bible, correctly translated, is, "The head one of the gods brought forth the gods."

In the King Follett Discourse, Joseph Smith said, "I shall comment on the very first Hebrew word in the Bible; I will make a comment on the very first sentence of the history of creation in the Bible—*Berosheit*. I want to analyze the word. *Baith*—in, by, through, and everything else. *Rosh*—the head, *Sheit*—grammatical termination. When the inspired man wrote it, he did not put the *baith* there. An old Jew without any authority added the word; he thought it too bad to begin to talk about the head! It read first, 'The head one of the gods brought forth the gods.' That is the true meaning of the words. *Baurau* signifies to bring forth. If you do not believe it, you do not believe the learned man of God. Learned men can teach you no more than what I have told you.

Thus the head God brought forth the gods in the grand council."

It is recorded in Mormon history that Joseph Smith was not a well-educated man. He had little public education as a boy, and no advanced education in his later years. Therefore, his understanding of languages such as Hebrew is regarded as being insight from the Lord.

Former Mormon President D.H. Wells said of Smith, "It seemed to me that he advanced principles that neither he nor any other man could have obtained except from the source of all wisdom—the Lord himself. I soon discovered that he was not what the world termed a well-read or an educated man; then where could he have got this knowledge and understanding, that so far surpassed all I had ever witnessed, unless it had come from heaven?"[20]

In the Pearl of Great Price, Smith attempted to correct what he believed to be an error in the translation of Genesis 1:1. Abraham 4:1 reads, "And

---

[20] Journal of Discourses, vol 12, pg 72. If one were to examine the original printing of the Book of Mormon, they would come to the opposite conclusion. According to former Mormons Jerald and Sandra Tanner, nearly 4,000 corrections have been made since that first edition. Most changes were corrections in spelling and grammar, but some had historical, theological and doctrinal implications. They wrote, "When a person examines the unchanged text of the 1830 (original) edition of the Book of Mormon, it becomes very obvious that it was written by someone without a great deal of education" (*The Changing World of Mormonism*, Moody Press, 1981, pg 128-133).

then the Lord said: Let us go down. And they went down at the beginning, and they, that is the Gods, organized and formed the heavens and the earth."

What the Bible Says:

Genesis 1:1 reads, "In the beginning, God created the heavens and the earth." That is the correct translation. It has been correct for thousands of years. Remember, the Mormons believe the Bible is only God's word "as far as it is translated correctly." As we commonly know Genesis 1:1, it was apparently not correct according Joseph Smith, who changed the Bible to mean what he wanted it to mean.

Without needing a lesson in Hebrew, the classic rendering of Genesis 1:1 can be affirmed by other Scriptures. The prophet Jeremiah said, "The gods who did not make the heavens and the earth shall perish from the earth and from under the heavens" (Jeremiah 10:11). In other words, "the gods" did not do anything in the beginning. The true God created the heavens and the earth on his own.

In John's gospel, we read, "In the beginning was the Word, and the Word was with God, and the Word was God. He was in the beginning with God. All things were made through him, and without him was not any thing made that was made" (John 1:1-3).

Isaiah 44:24 reads, "Thus says the Lord, your Redeemer, who formed you from the womb: 'I am the Lord, who made all things, who alone stretched out the heavens, who spread out the earth by myself.'"

Psalm 33:6 and 9 reads, "By the word of the Lord the heavens were made, and by the breath of his mouth all their host. For he spoke and it came to be; he commanded, and it stood firm."

2) God did not create the world from nothing but from pre-existing matter.

In the King Follett Discourse, Smith said, "Now, I ask all who hear me, why the learned men who are preaching salvation, say that God created the heavens and the earth out of nothing? The reason is, that they are unlearned in the things of God, and have not the gift of the Holy Ghost; they account it blasphemy in any one to contradict their idea. If you tell them that God made the world out of something, they will call you a fool. But I am learned, and know more than all the world put together."[21]

Smith went on to explain that the Hebrew word for create, *baurau*, does not mean to create out of nothing. Rather, it means to organize, "the same as a man would organize materials and build a ship. Hence we infer that God had materials to organize the world out of chaos—chaotic matter, which is element, and in which dwells all the glory. Element had an existence from the time he had. The pure principles of element are principles which can never

---

[21] Yes, Smith said he knew more than all the world put together.

be destroyed; they may be organized and reorganized, but not destroyed. They had no beginning and can have no end."

What the Bible Says:

Again, a knowledge of Hebrew is not necessary to know that Smith was wrong. Romans 4:17 says that God "calls into existence the things that do not exist." Hebrews 11:3 reads, "By faith we understand that the universe was created by the word of God, so that what is seen was not made out of things that are visible."

Jeremiah 32:17 reads, "Ah, Lord God! It is you who have made the heavens and the earth by your great power and by your outstretched arm! Nothing is too hard for you." Colossians 1:16 reads, "For by him all things were created, in heaven and on earth, visible and invisible, whether thrones or dominions or rulers or authorities—all things were created through him and for him."

As God can create, God can also destroy. Psalm 37:38 reads, "But transgressors shall be altogether destroyed." In 2 Thessalonians 2:8, we read, "And then the lawless one will be revealed, whom the Lord Jesus will kill with the breath of his mouth and bring to nothing by the appearance of his coming." James 4:12 reads, "There is only one lawgiver and judge, he who is able to save and to destroy." And in 1 Corinthians 15:25-26, "For he must reign until he has put all his enemies under his feet. The last enemy to be destroyed is death."

Smith's tendency to quarrel over words is addressed in Scripture as well. In 2 Timothy 2:14, we are told "not to quarrel about words, which does no good, but only ruins the hearers."

3) God the Father is not eternal, but was born as a baby, and is a man of flesh and bones.

In the King Follett Discourse, Smith preached, "We have imagined and supposed that God was God from all eternity. I will refute that idea, and take away the veil, so that you may see."

He said, "God himself was once as we are now, and is an exalted man, and sits enthroned in yonder heavens! That is the great secret. If the veil were rent today, and the great God who holds this world in its orbit, and who upholds all the worlds and all things by his power, was to make himself visible—I say, if you were to see him today, you would see him like a man in form—like yourselves in all the person, image, and very form as a man."[22]

In another sermon, Smith said, "If Jesus had a Father, can we not believe that he had a father also? I despise the idea of being scared to death at such a

---

[22] The King Follett Discourse is perhaps the most revealing piece of Latter-Day Saint history in understanding what the Mormons believe about God. Smith preached at the funeral of Mormon Elder King Follett on April 7, 1844. It was one of the last sermons he preached before he died that following June.

doctrine, for the Bible is full of it."[23]

It is reported that Smith also said, "That which is without body or parts is nothing. There is no other God in heaven but that God who has flesh and bones."[24] Doctrine and Covenants 130:22 says, "The Father has a body of flesh and bones as tangible as man's; the Son also; but the Holy Ghost has not a body of flesh and bones, but is a personage of Spirit. Were it not so, the Holy Ghost could not dwell in us."

What the Bible Says:

The Bible has much to say about the eternal nature of God. Psalm 90:2 says, "Before the mountains were brought forth, or ever you had formed the earth and the world, from everlasting to everlasting, you are God." Deuteronomy 33:27 says, "The eternal God is your dwelling place, and underneath are the everlasting arms." And in 1 Timothy 1:17, "To the King of the ages, immortal, invisible, the only God, be honor and glory forever and ever. Amen."

Regarding God's appearance as that of a man's, the Bible says quite the opposite. In John 4:23-24, Jesus said, "The hour is coming, and is now here, when the true worshipers will worship the Father in spirit and truth, for the Father is seeking such people to worship him. God is spirit, and those who wor-

---

[23] Known as the Sermon in the Grove, June 16, 1844.
[24] Extracts from William Clayton's Private Book, pg 7.

ship him must worship in spirit and truth." In 1 Samuel 15:29 and Numbers 23:19, it is explicitly stated: "God is not a man."

Joseph Smith came up with this idea of God being flesh and bone by twisting the meaning of 1 Corinthians 15:50. There Paul said, "I tell you this, brothers: flesh and blood cannot inherit the kingdom of God, nor does the perishable inherit the imperishable." Therefore, according to Smith, God cannot be flesh and *blood*, but apparently flesh and *bone* qualify for eternal existence. (Do I really need to point out that flesh and bone are still perishable?)

The point Paul was making was this: In our perishable bodies, we cannot stand in the presence of the glory of God. Our flesh would melt, our bones crumble into dust. The physical cannot enter into the spiritual. One must be resurrected to a new body, which Paul clarified in the previous verses: "Just as we have borne the image of the man of dust," meaning Adam, "we shall also bear the image of the man of heaven," meaning Jesus (1 Corinthians 15:49).

We read in 1 John 3:2, "Beloved, we are God's children now, and what we will be has not yet appeared; but we know that when he appears we shall be like him, because we shall see him as he is." Not that we will become gods, but our bodies will be made to be like his so we can live in his presence. Paul said that God "will transform our lowly body to be like his glorious body, by the power that enables him even to subject all things to himself" (Philippians 3:21).

Smith constantly contorted the scriptures into a different meaning. Christians and Mormons will often have the same lexicon, using the same words, terms, and names, but they will have completely different meanings.

Unlike the Mormon god, the true God is eternal. He has no beginning and no end.

4) God is just one of many gods.

In the King Follett Discourse, Smith said, "The head God called together the gods, and they sat in the grand council. The grand councilors sat in yonder heavens and contemplated the creation of the worlds that were created at that time."

In his attempt to define the Trinity, Smith said, "I have always declared God to be a distinct personage, Jesus Christ a separate and distinct personage from God the Father, and that the Holy Ghost was a distinct personage and a Spirit: and these three constitute three distinct personages and three gods."[25] By this definition, Smith declared that God and Jesus and the Holy Spirit are not three persons in one God, but three different gods.

In one of his last sermons, Smith said, "Many men say there is one God; the Father, the Son, and the Holy Ghost are only one God and I say that is a

---

[25] History of the Church, 6:474.

strange God anyhow—three in one, and one in three! It is a curious organization." He went on, "All are crammed into one God, according to sectarianism. It would make the biggest God in all the world. He would be a wonderfully big God—he would be a giant or a monster."

Mormons believe not only in many gods, but many goddesses (Doctrine and Covenants, 132:19-20). Some Mormon apologists have argued for an infinite number of gods in an infinite number of universes. Regardless, the only three gods that are to be worshiped by us on earth are Elohim, his son, Jesus, and the Holy Ghost.

What the Bible Says:

Deuteronomy 4:35 reads, "To you it was shown, that you might know that the Lord is God; there is no other besides him." Deuteronomy 6:4 reads, "Hear, O Israel: The Lord our God, the Lord is one." Jesus repeated this verse again in Mark 12:29. Psalm 86:10 reads, "For you are great and do wondrous things; you alone are God."

The exclusivity of God is clearly stated in the Scriptures. We read in 1 Corinthians 8:4, "There is no God but one." Even the demons believe there is only one God. James 2:19 says, "You believe that God is one; you do well. Even the demons believe—and shudder!" To believe there is more than one God is to believe worse things than the demons believe!

Isaiah 43:10-11 says, "'You are my witnesses,' declares the Lord, 'and my servant whom I have chosen, that you may know and believe me and understand that I am he. Before me no god was formed, nor shall there be any after me. I, I am the Lord, and besides me there is no savior.'"

Isaiah 44:6-8 says, "Thus says the Lord, the King of Israel and his Redeemer, the Lord of hosts: 'I am the first and I am the last; besides me there is no god. Who is like me? Let him proclaim it. Let him declare and set it before me, since I appointed an ancient people. Let them declare what is to come, and what will happen. Fear not, nor be afraid; have I not told you from of old and declared it? And you are my witnesses! Is there a God besides me? There is no Rock; I know not any."

Isaiah 46:9-10 says, "I am God, and there is no other; I am God, and there is none like me, declaring the end from the beginning and from ancient times things not yet done, saying, 'My counsel shall stand, and I will accomplish my purpose.'"

5) We are all the literal sons and daughters of God, begotten from Heavenly Father and Heavenly Mother.

In *Gospel Principles*, at the start of chapter 2, it says, "God is not only our Ruler and Creator; He is also our Heavenly Father. All men and women are literally the sons and daughters of God. 'Man, as a spirit, was begotten and born of heavenly parents, and reared to maturity in the eternal mansions of the Father, prior to coming upon the earth in a temporal body' (Teachings of Presidents of the Church: Joseph F. Smith [1998], 335)."

According to Mormon theology, we all started out as spirit children, conceived through celestial sex between Heavenly Father and Heavenly Mother. Elaine Anderson Cannon, eighth president of the Young Women organization of the LDS, said that Heavenly Father is like God "in glory, perfection, compassion, wisdom, and holiness."

In the Encyclopedia of Mormonism, she wrote, "Latter-day Saints believe that all the people of earth who lived or will live are actual spiritual offspring of God the Eternal Father" and that "Heavenly Mother shares parenthood with the Heavenly Father."

Cannon went on to say that the teaching of Heavenly Mother originates with Joseph Smith as early as 1839. "Out of his teaching came a hymn that Latter-day Saints learn, sing, quote, and cherish, 'O My Father' by Eliza R. Snow. President Wilford Woodruff called it a revelation." She quoted the lyric of Hymn No. 292:

In the heavens are parents single?
No, the thought makes reason stare!
Truth is reason; truth eternal
Tells me I've a mother there.
When I leave this frail existence,
When I lay this mortal by,

Father, Mother, may I meet you
In your royal courts on high?

Cannon continued, "In 1909 the First Presidency, under Joseph F. Smith, issued a statement on the origin of man that teaches that 'man, as a spirit, was begotten and born of heavenly parents, and reared to maturity in the eternal mansions of the Father,' as an 'offspring of celestial parentage,' and further teaches that 'all men and women are in the similitude of the universal Father and Mother, and are literally the sons and daughters of Deity'" (pg. 961).

What the Bible Says:
Romans 8:15 says, "For you did not receive the spirit of slavery to fall back into fear, but you have received the Spirit of adoption as sons, by whom we cry, 'Abba! Father!'" Galatians 4:5 says that through Christ we have received "adoption as sons." Ephesians 1:5 says, "He predestined us for adoption as sons through Jesus Christ, according to the purpose of his will."

Our being received as children of God is through a spiritual adoption. In no way are we literally begotten through celestial sex between God and a goddess. Furthermore, we are not born children of God, but we are *born again* to become children of God through Christ.

John 1:12 says, "But to all who did receive him, who believed in his name, he gave the right to become children of God." Jesus said to Nicodemus, "Truly, truly, I say to you, unless one is born again he cannot see the kingdom of God" (John 3:3).

All people are either children of the devil—meaning that their ways follow in the ways of Satan—or they are children of God—meaning that their ways follow in the ways of God. We read in 1 John 3:9-10, "No one born of God makes a practice of sinning, for God's seed abides in him, and he cannot keep on sinning because he has been born of God. By this it is evident who are the children of God, and who are the children of the devil: whoever does not practice righteousness is not of God, nor is the one who does not love his brother."

There is only one God, not multiple gods. So there can be no goddess called Heavenly Mother.

6) God lives on another planet near the star Kolob, and there are many other inhabited worlds.

According to Doctrine and Covenants 76:24, through Jesus, "the worlds are and were created, and the inhabitants thereof are begotten sons and daughters of God."

In the Pearl of Great Price, Abraham 3:2-3 reads, "And I saw the stars, that they were very great, and that one of them was nearest unto the throne of God; and there were many great ones which were near unto it; And the Lord said unto me: These are the governing ones; and the name of the great one is Kolob, because it is near unto me, for I am the Lord thy God: I have set this one to govern all those which belong to the same order as that upon which thou standest."

Apostle Joseph Fielding Smith wrote, "We are not the only people that the Lord has created. We have brothers and sisters on other earths. They look like us because they, too, are the children of God and were created in his image, for they are also his offspring."[26]

Supposedly, Joseph Smith claimed that the moon was inhabited by moon people. Oliver B. Huntington wrote, "As far back as 1837, I know that [Smith] said the moon was inhabited by men and women the same as this earth, and that they lived to a greater age than we do—that they live generally to near the age of 1,000 years."[27]

Some Mormon apologists dispute this claim as accurate since it came from a third party. But later presidents Hyrum Smith and Brigham Young openly affirmed that people lived on the moon.

Young doubled-down on his claim that there were moon-people, and said there were also "inhabitants of the sun. Do you think it is inhabited? I rather think it is. Do you think there is any life there? No question of it; it was not made in vain. It was made to give light to those who dwell upon it, and to other planets; and so will this earth when it is to be

---

[26] Doctrines of Salvation, 1:62.
[27] Young Women's Journal, 3:263-264, March, 1892

celestialized."[28] [29]

What the Bible Says:

The Bible says God is in heaven (1 Kings 8:49, Matthew 6:9) and also that he dwells among man (2 Corinthians 6:16, Ephesians 2:22). As has been mentioned, God is spirit and does not live in some physical place. When Solomon consecrated the temple, he said, "But will God indeed dwell on the earth? Behold, heaven and the heaven of heavens cannot contain you; how much less this house that I have built!" (1 Kings 8:27).

What's the harm with imagining that God might dwell on another planet? First of all, the Mormon faith doesn't present this as theory or make-believe. They present it as truth, so it's a lie. Secondly, the Bible says not to go beyond what is written (1 Corinthians 4:6). The Apostle Paul told Timothy to avoid irreverent silly myths (1 Timothy 4:7) and irreverent babble and contradictions of what is falsely called

---

[28] Journal of Discourses 13:271.

[29] In 1995, attempting to cover for the legitimacy of their prophets, a Mormon publication entitled *One-Minute Answers to Anti-Mormon Questions* defended the claim that people lived on the moon: "At the present time, man has no scientific or revealed knowledge of whether or not there are inhabitants on the earth's moon. The fact that a handful of astronauts didn't see any inhabitants in the tiny area they viewed when they landed on the moon decades ago certainly gives no definitive information, any more than visitors to earth who might land in barren Death Valley would have any idea of the billions of inhabitants elsewhere."

"knowledge" (1 Timothy 6:20).

He said that if a man teaches a different doctrine than the one that agrees with the sound words of our Lord Jesus Christ, "he is puffed up with conceit and understands nothing. He has an unhealthy craving for controversy and for quarrels about words, which produce envy, dissension, slander, evil suspicions, and constant friction among people who are depraved in mind and deprived of the truth, imagining that godliness is a means of gain" (1 Timothy 6:3-5).

7) God was once a sinner like us and completed a process of becoming divine.

In the King Follett Discourse, Smith said Jesus laid his life down as just the Father did and worked out His kingdom with fear and trembling as he saw his Father do. He said, "Here, then, is eternal life — to know the only wise and true God; and you have got to learn how to be gods yourselves, and to be kings and priests to God, the same as all gods have done before you."

Apostle Orson Hyde said, "God our Heavenly Father was perhaps once a child, and mortal like we are, and rose step by step in the scale of progress, in the school of advancement; has moved forward and overcome, until he has arrived at the point where he is now."[30]

Apostle Bruce McConkie wrote, "The Father is a

---

[30] Journal of Discourses 1:123

glorified, perfected, resurrected, exalted man who worked out his own salvation by obedience to the same laws he has given to us so that we may do the same."[31] Only those who have died need resurrected, and only those who have fallen need salvation.

Truth be told, there are a few Mormons that don't agree with this idea that God went through a process of becoming divine. They would refer to passages like Moroni 7:22 that echoes Psalm 90:2 saying that God is "from everlasting to everlasting." Moroni 8:18 says, "For I know that God is not a partial God, neither a changeable being; but he is unchangeable from all eternity to all eternity."

Mormon teaching changed even during the lifetime of Joseph Smith. His famous King Follett Discourse, when he declared that God was once a man, was preached in 1844. But the Book of Mormon, first published in 1830, does not appear to share the same teaching. That God is an exalted man is a doctrine that came about as Mormon theology and cosmology evolved.

In 1844, Joseph Smith said, "We have imagined and supposed that God was God from all eternity. I will refute that idea, and take away the veil, so that you may see." But in 1830, Joseph Smith said, "He is unchangeable from all eternity to all eternity." Smith refuted himself.

Nevertheless, later LDS apostles firmly believed

---

[31] A New Witness for the Articles of Faith, pg 64.

and taught that God was once a sinner like us. They will reinterpret passages like Moroni 7:22 and 8:18 to fit that understanding. LDS apostle James E. Talmage said, "As man is, God once was; as God is, man may be."[32]

What the Bible Says:

James 1:13 says, "God cannot be tempted with evil." If God cannot be tempted, there is no adversity for him to overcome. Therefore, there is no process through which he can get better than he already is. He is already perfect.

Unfortunately, a Mormon apologist will likely not settle for that argument. They will say that God is perfect *now*, and any reference in the Bible to his incorruptibility describes his present state. He became perfect, but has not always been perfect. So we must consider passages that talk about how God has *always been* perfect.

In Revelation 4, the Apostle John saw a vision of a throne in heaven and on each side are four creatures. "Day and night they never cease to say, 'Holy, holy, holy, is the Lord God Almighty, who was and is and is to come!'" (Revelation 4:8). Psalm 119:142 says, "Your righteousness is righteous forever, and your law is true." God is holy and righteous and always has been. He is always without sin or any imperfection.

---

[32] Articles of Faith, Chapter 24, pg. 430-431.

Numbers 23:19 says, "God is not a man, that he should lie, or a son of man, that he should change his mind. He has said, and will he not do it? Or has he spoken, and will he not fulfill it?" Job 34:10 and 12 reads, "Far be it from God that he should do wickedness, and from the Almighty that he should do wrong. Of a truth, God will not do wickedly, and the Almighty will not pervert justice."

God did not obey a set of laws which he then passed on to us, for he is the originator of that law. Psalm 18:30 says, "This God—his way is perfect; the word of the Lord proves true; he is a shield for all those who take refuge in him." And in Psalm 19:7, "The law of the Lord is perfect."

No law governs God. Psalm 135:6 says, "Whatsoever the Lord pleased, that did he in heaven, and in earth, in the seas, and all deep places." And Psalm 115:3, "Our God is in the heavens; he does all that he pleases." Job 34:13 reads, "Who gave him charge over the earth, and who laid on him the whole world?" And Job 21:22, "Shall any teach God knowledge? Seeing he judgeth those that are high."

We read in 1 Corinthians 15:56, "The sting of death is sin, and the power of sin is the law." Hebrews 7:19 says, "For the law made nothing perfect." God could not have attained perfection by obedience since nothing is perfected by obedience to the law. We are perfected by God (1 Peter 5:10).

8) You can become a god yourself.

In the King Follett Discourse, Smith said, "Here, then, is eternal life — to know the only wise and true God. And you have got to learn how to be Gods yourselves — to be kings and priests to God, the same as all Gods have done — by going from a small degree to another, from grace to grace, from exaltation to exaltation, until you are able to sit in glory as do those who sit enthroned in everlasting power."

In Doctrine and Covenants, he also wrote the following: "And again, verily I say unto you, if a man marry a wife by my word, which is my law, and by the new and everlasting covenant, and it is sealed unto them by the Holy Spirit of promise, by him who is anointed, unto whom I have appointed this power and the keys of this priesthood; and it shall be said unto them — Ye shall come forth in the first resurrection; and if it be after the first resurrection, in the next resurrection; and shall inherit thrones, kingdoms, principalities, and powers, dominions, all heights and depths — then shall it be written in the Lamb's Book of Life, that he shall commit no murder whereby to shed innocent blood, and if ye abide in my covenant, and commit no murder whereby to shed innocent blood, it shall be done unto them in all things whatsoever my servant hath put upon them, in time, and through all eternity; and shall be of full force when they are out of the world; and they shall pass by the angels, and the gods, which are set there, to their exaltation and glory in all things, as hath been sealed upon their heads, which glory shall be a fullness and a continuation of the seeds forever and ever.

"Then shall they be gods, because they have no end; therefore shall they be from everlasting to everlasting, because they continue; then shall they be above all, because all things are subject unto them. Then shall they be gods, because they have all power, and the angels are subject to them."[33]

What the Bible Says:

The idea that we can become gods or like God was Satan's lie in the Garden of Eden. In Genesis 3:1-5, the serpent said to the woman, "Did God actually say, 'You shall not eat of any tree in the garden'?"

The woman replied, "We may eat of the fruit of the trees in the garden, but God said, 'You shall not eat of the fruit of the tree that is in the midst of the garden, neither shall you touch it, lest you die.'"

The serpent said to the woman, "You will not surely die. For God knows that when you eat of it your eyes will be opened, and *you will be like God*, knowing good and evil."

So she took of the fruit and ate it, and then gave it to her husband, who was also with her, and he ate. And their eyes were opened. They were filled with shame. And man fell from God.

---

[33] Doctrine and Covenants, 132:19-20.

In the King Follett Discourse, Joseph Smith said that if he failed to find out the character of God and reveal it, it would become his duty "to renounce all further pretensions to revelations and inspirations, or to be a prophet" and that all should consider him "a false teacher."

By his own words, so he should be considered as such.

What the Mormons Believe About

Jesus Christ

1) Jesus is a created spirit, the firstborn of Heavenly Father and Heavenly Mother.

Recall that in the previous chapter, it was mentioned that Mormons believe we are all spirit children begotten of Heavenly Father and Heavenly Mother.[34] The firstborn of these spirit children was Jesus Christ.

According to the First Presidency and the Quorum of the Twelve Apostles,[35] "God the Eternal Father, whom we designate by the exalted name-title 'Elohim,' is the literal Parent of our Lord and Savior Jesus Christ and of the spirits of the human race. Elohim is the Father in every sense in which Jesus Christ is so designated, and distinctively He is the

---

[34] Encyclopedia of Mormonism, pg. 961.
[35] The LDS church is governed by fifteen apostles. The oldest apostle is the President, and he has chosen two other apostles to be his council. They are referred to as the First Presidency. The rest make up the Quorum of the Twelve Apostles.

Father of spirits."[36]

Joseph Fielding Smith said, "Among the spirit children of Elohim, the first-born was and is Jehovah, or Jesus Christ, to whom all others are juniors."[37] Bruce McConkie said that Jesus was the first spirit to be born in the heavens.[38] In the Book of Mormon, Alma 36:17 refers to Jesus as *a* Son of God, not *the* Son of God.[39]

What the Bible Says:

Colossians 1:15-17 says that Jesus "is the image of the invisible God, the firstborn of every creature: For by him were all things created, that are in heaven, and that are in earth, visible and invisible, whether thrones, or dominions, or principalities, or powers: all things were created by him, and for him: And he is before all things, and by him all things consist."

---

[36] Improvement Era, August, 1916, pg. 934-942.

[37] Gospel Doctrine, pg. 70.

[38] Mormon Doctrine, pg. 129.

[39] The Mormons believe that the Father's true name is Elohim, and they believe that Jesus's true name is Jehovah. All mentions to Jehovah in the Old Testament are specifically referring to Jesus. The pronunciation and spelling of Yahweh (YHWH) as "Jehovah" first appeared in the 16th century and was popularized by William Tyndale and English translations of the Bible such as the Geneva Bible and the King James Version. Though it's okay to refer to God as Jehovah, it can't possibly be his real name. The Jehovah's Witnesses are another group who will claim that God's true name is Jehovah, which is false.

Now, this is a passage that Mormons (and also Jehovah's Witnesses) use to explain that Jesus is a created spirit. After all, it says right there: he is "the firstborn." So Jesus was the first *born,* right?

But if that's what the passage was saying, then Jesus could not have created all things, for he himself is created. Note that it's not just the earth he created, but all things visible and invisible. John 1:3 says, "All things were made by him; and without him was not any thing made that was made."

What Colossians 1:15 means by saying Jesus is the firstborn of all creation is that God the Father has given him all the rights of the firstborn—all things belong to Christ. Hebrews 1:2 puts it another way: God has appointed him "heir of all things."

The Mormon idea that God didn't create anything but just rearranged pre-existing matter also comes into conflict with this passage. God, specifically Jesus Christ, created everything visible and invisible. He is not a created spirit, nor did matter exist before him.

John 1, Colossians 1, Hebrews 1, and Revelation 1 make clear: Jesus is the eternal Creator God.[40]

---

[40] The Mormon church has never produced a meaningful exposition of any book of the Bible. If they tried, it would destroy their religion. Referencing out-of-context passages is the only way they manage to press or maintain their beliefs in any convincing way.

2) The second-born son of God the Father was Satan, the brother of Jesus.

According to the LDS teacher's manual entitled *Gospel Principles*, it says, "We needed a Savior to pay for our sins and teach us how to return to our Heavenly Father. Our Father said, 'Whom shall I send?' (Abraham 3:27). Two of our brothers offered to help. Our oldest brother, Jesus Christ, who was then called Jehovah, said, 'Here am I, send me' (Abraham 3:27)."

The chapter continues, "Satan, who was called Lucifer,[41] also came, saying, 'Behold, here am I, send me, I will be thy son, and I will redeem all mankind, that one soul shall not be lost, and surely I will do it; wherefore give me thine honor' (Moses 4:1). Satan wanted to force us all to do his will. Under his plan, we would not be allowed to choose. He would take away the freedom of choice that our Father had given us."

The manual goes on, "After hearing both sons speak, Heavenly Father said, 'I will send the first' (Abraham 3:27). Jesus Christ was chosen and

---

[41] Just as Jehovah is not Jesus's true name, Lucifer is not Satan's true name. The name comes from Isaiah 14:12 where the prophet compares the fall of the king of Babylon to the fall of Satan. In the King James Version, the name Lucifer appears, the Latin word for "daystar" or "morning star." The same word appears in Job 11:17 and 2 Peter 1:19 of the Latin Vulgate, but those passages do not mention Satan. When the Latin was translated into English, "lucifer" was translated as a proper noun. More modern translations don't include "Lucifer" as it isn't Satan's true name.

foreordained to be our Savior."

This means that you also are a literal brother or sister of Jesus—and Satan. This also means that Jesus is not the true God, but one of many gods, and Satan could also be called a god.

What the Bible Says:

As has been established, Jesus is a divine, un-caused, eternal being. He was not created but is the Creator of all things, visible and invisible, princi-palities and powers. Satan was one of those invisible beings God created.

In Ezekiel 28, the prophet compares the fall of the king of Tyre to the fall of Satan. He said, "You were the signet of perfection, full of wisdom and perfect in beauty. You were in Eden, the garden of God; every precious stone was your carving... On the day that you were created they were prepared. You were an anointed guardian cherub" (v.12-14). So Satan was an angel before he rebelled against God and was cast from heaven, taking a third of the angels with him who became the demons (Revelation 12:4).

The Bible says that the reason Jesus came was to destroy the works of the devil (1 John 3:8). He will come back again and destroy Satan "with the breath of his mouth" (2 Thessalonians 2:8). In other words, Satan's defeat will be effortless—*poof*, and he's done. The devil is not Jesus' brother nor does he have any kind of power equal to his. There are angels that have been given more power than Satan has (see Daniel 12:1 and Revelation 20:1-3).

3) Mary was not a virgin when Jesus was born.

In the Book of Mormon, Nephi sees the virgin Mary about 600 years before the birth of Christ. He wrote, "And he said unto me: Behold, the virgin whom thou seest is the mother of the Son of God, after the manner of the flesh" (1 Nephi 11:18).

Alma 7:10 reads, "And behold, he shall be born of Mary, at Jerusalem[42] which is the land of our fore-fathers, she being a virgin, a precious and chosen vessel, who shall be overshadowed and conceive by the power of the Holy Ghost, and bring forth a son, yea, even the Son of God."

Yet later Mormon doctrines would conflict with this idea of Mary being a virgin. Brigham Young outright denied that Mary conceived by the Holy Spirit: "Now remember from this time forth, and forever, that Jesus Christ was not begotten by the Holy Ghost."[43]

Joseph Fielding Smith said the same, and clarified, "Christ was begotten of God. He was not born

---

[42] Another error in the Book of Mormon claiming Jesus was born in Jerusalem, not Bethlehem. Mormon apologists say that "Jerusalem" describes the region. But even Micah 5:2 prophesied the very city where Jesus would be born. Micah was written about 700 B.C. while Alma 7 claims to have been first written in 83 B.C. Why couldn't Alma get the right place?

[43] Journal of Discourses, vol 1, pg. 51.

without the aid of Man, and that Man was God!"[44] He also said, "The birth of the Savior was a natural occurrence unattended by any degree of mysticism, and the Father God was the literal parent of Jesus in the flesh as well as in the spirit."[45]

This literally means that God the Father, Elohim, came down to earth and had sex with Mary so she would conceive and have Jesus. Bruce McConkie offered an explanation as to why Mary being called a "virgin," as in Alma 7:10, was still accurate: "For our present purposes, suffice it to say that our Lord was born of a virgin, which is fitting and proper, and also natural, since the Father of the Child was an immortal being."[46]

So Elohim had sex with Mary—who, remember, is one of his literal children which makes their union an act of incest—and impregnated her with Jesus, but she was still a virgin and Jesus was still virgin-born because God is immortal and she did not have sex with a mortal man.

According to Mormon apologetics, if the first time you had sexual intercourse was with a being who was immortal, you would still come out of the experience a virgin, as Mary remained a virgin after she had sex with her Father, Elohim.[47]

---

[44] Doctrines of Salvation, 1:18.
[45] Religious Truths Defined, pg. 44.
[46] The Promised Messiah, pg. 466.
[47] Robert Millet, in his apologetic book *A Different Jesus?: The Christ of the Latter-day Saints*, tried to wave off this idea of Elohim

What the Bible Says:

Matthew 1:18 says, "Now the birth of Jesus Christ took place in this way. When his mother Mary had been betrothed to Joseph, before they came together she was found to be with child from the Holy Spirit." There is simply no way around it: the Bible says Jesus was conceived by the Holy Spirit.

At the start of Luke's gospel, the angel Gabriel came to Mary and said she would be with child. "And Mary said to the angel, 'How will this be, since I am a virgin?' And the angel answered her, 'The Holy Spirit will come upon you, and the power of the Most High will overshadow you; therefore the child to be born will be called holy—the Son of God'" (Luke 1:34-35).

Mormonism simply does not understand the theological implications in the virgin birth. Because of Adam's sin against God, all things were subjected to futility (Romans 8:20). Romans 5:12 says that all sin came into the world through one man, Adam, and death through sin, so death spread to all men because all sinned. All who are born in the line of Adam are born into sin.[48]

---

having sex with Mary by saying that we do not know how Jesus' conception was accomplished. However, more authoritative Mormon teachers have been quite clear: "Christ was begotten by an Immortal Father in the same way that mortal men are begotten by mortal fathers" (McConkie, Mormon Doctrine).

[48] Mormons reject the doctrine of Original Sin or ancestral sin,

However, Jesus was not born in the line of Adam because he was not conceived by the seed of a man. It could be argued, "Well, Mormons don't believe he was born of the seed of a man either. He was conceived of by God!" But we just read from Joseph Fielding Smith that Jesus was conceived by a man, though that man was God.

Remember from the previous chapter: Mormons believe God is an exalted man who became perfect but was not always perfect. He sinned and died as every man sins and dies; therefore, it cannot be said of him that he is without sin. He, like fallen man, was born with a sin nature.

The Bible says that Jesus was and is sinless and never knew any sin. Hebrews 4:15 says "he did not sin;" 2 Corinthians 5:21 says he "knew no sin;" 1 John 3:5 says, "in him there is no sin;" and 1 Peter 2:22 says, "He committed no sin and no deceit was found in his mouth."

Jesus did something no man ever did nor will any man ever do—he lived a perfect, sinless life. He accomplished this not simply because he didn't *commit* sin, but because he was not *conceived* in sin by the seed of sinful man. He was the perfect Lamb without blemish or defect (1 Peter 1:19). He did not merely *become* a perfect sacrifice. He was *born* the perfect sacrifice. He is the only man ever to not have

---

that all who are born of Adam inherit his sin nature, as the Bible says.

been born of the seed of man, so he is the only perfect man to have ever lived.

The reason why the virgin birth matters is because if Jesus was born of the seed of a man, he stands condemned since Adam would be his federal head. All who are conceived and born natural are under the federal headship of Adam, as Romans 5 explains. But Jesus was not conceived of by man, even an exalted man. He was conceived by the Holy Spirit.

In Christ's *active* obedience—his sinless actions—he fulfilled the Law and the Prophets, having kept the law perfectly and was righteous. In his *passive* obedience—his sinless nature—he took upon himself the death that we owed to God but couldn't pay because of our sinful nature. Christ imputes upon us his righteousness, and imputed upon him was our sinfulness, as the Scriptures teach—"For our sake He made Him to be sin who knew no sin, so that in Him we might become the righteousness of God" (2 Corinthians 5:21).[49] Therefore, we are able to live in a way that is pleasing to God and stand before him justified because of the righteousness of Christ he has given to us.

The incarnation of Christ—the Son of God became flesh, conceived by the Holy Spirit, born of the virgin Mary—is an essential biblical doctrine. To deny it is heresy. We are all born under the federal

---

[49] This is a doctrine called Double Imputation.

headship of Adam; we are *born again* under the federal headship of Christ, who takes away our sin.

4) Jesus, like his Father before him, became God through obedience.

In the King Follett Discourse, Joseph Smith said, "What did Jesus do? Why, I do the things I saw my Father do when worlds came rolling into existence. My Father worked out His kingdom with fear and trembling, and I must do the same."

Joseph Fielding Smith said, "Jesus, like all other Gods before Him, had to become a God. He is the literal Son of God like we are children of God, but He's without sin."[50]

Bruce McConkie said, "Jesus kept the commandments of his Father and thereby worked out his own salvation, and also set an example as to the way and means whereby all men may be saved."[51]

He also said, "Christ the Word, the Firstborn, had of course attained unto the status of Godhood while yet in pre-existence."[52] In *Mormon Doctrine*, he wrote, "By obedience and devotion to the truth he attained that pinnacle of intelligence which ranked him as a God, as the Lord Omnipotent, while yet in his pre-existent state" (pg. 129).

---

[50] The Teachings of the Prophet Joseph Smith, pg. 346.
[51] The Mortal Messiah, Vol. 4, pg. 434.
[52] What Mormons Think of Christ, pg. 36

What the Bible Says:

Hebrews 7:16 says plainly that Jesus is our High Priest, "not after the law of a carnal commandment, but after the power of an endless life." Verse 21 says, "The Lord sware and will not repent, Thou art a priest forever," and verse 24 says, "because he continueth ever, hath an unchangeable priesthood."

Hebrews 7:28 says, "For the law maketh men high priests which have infirmity; but the word of the oath, which was since the law, maketh the Son, who is consecrated forevermore." The oath was made in Psalm 110:4 (quoted in verse 21) and came after the Mosaic law, setting aside the previous Mosaic priesthood by making the Son of God the eternal High Priest.

Jesus has existed eternally with God. In John 17:5, he said, "And now, Father, glorify me in your own presence with the glory that I had with you before the world existed." Hebrews 1:8 says, "But of the Son he says, 'Your throne, O God, is forever and ever, the scepter of uprightness is the scepter of your kingdom.'"

The Bible says that Jesus, "though he was in the form of God, did not count equality with God a thing to be grasped, but emptied himself, by taking the form of a servant, being born in the likeness of men" (Philippians 2:6-7).[53]

In Revelation 1:8, Jesus describes himself as the

---

[53] Philippians 2:5-11 is often called the Hymn of Christ.

Alpha and Omega, the beginning and the end, and in verse 17 as the First and the Last. He did not become God—He is and has always been God.

5) The death of Jesus did not atone for all sins.

Doctrine and Covenants 42:18 says, "And now, behold, I speak unto the church. Thou shalt not kill; and he that kills shall not have forgiveness in this world, nor in the world to come."

Then 24-26 says, "Thou shalt not commit adultery; and he that committeth adultery, and repenteth not, shall be cast out. But he that has committed adultery and repents with all his heart, and forsaketh it, and doeth it no more, thou shalt forgive; But if he doeth it again, he shall not be forgiven, but shall be cast out."

So the blood of Christ does not atone for murder, and a person that commits adultery a second time shall not be forgiven.

Joseph Fielding Smith said, "Joseph Smith taught that there were certain sins so grievous that man may commit, that they will place the transgressors beyond the power of atonement of Christ. If these offenses are committed, then the blood of Christ will not cleanse them from their sins even though they repent. Therefore, their only hope is to have their own blood shed to atone, as far as possible, in their behalf."[54]

---

[54] Doctrines of Salvation, vol. 1, pg. 135.

Brigham Young said, "It is true that the blood of the Son of God was shed for sins through the fall and those committed by men, yet men can commit sins which it can never remit… There are sins that can be atoned for by an offering on the altar… And there are sins that the blood of a lamb… cannot remit, but they must be atoned for by the blood of the man."[55]

Young also said, "There is not a man or a woman who violates the covenants made with their God, that will not be required to pay the debt. The blood of Christ will never wipe that out, your own blood must atone for it."[56]

Bruce McConkie said, "But under certain circumstances there are some serious sins for which the cleansing of Christ does not operate, and the law of God is that men must then have their own blood shed to atone for their sins."[57]

What the Bible Says:

Romans 6:9-10 reads, "We know that Christ, being raised from the dead, will never die again; death no longer has dominion over him. For the death he died he died to sin, once for all," meaning *all sins.* Hebrews 7:27 says that Christ "has no need, like those high priests, to offer sacrifices daily, first

---

[55] Journal of Discourses, vol. 4, pg 53-54.

[56] Journal of Discourses, vol. 3, pg. 247.

[57] Mormon Doctrine, pg. 92. This is why the state of Utah is the only state in the Union to still sentence a person to death by firing squad for capital punishment.

for his own sins and then for those of the people, since he did this once for all when he offered up himself."

In Mark 3:28-29, Jesus said, "Truly, I say to you, all sins will be forgiven the children of man, and whatever blasphemies they utter, but whoever blasphemes against the Holy Spirit never has forgiveness, but is guilty of an eternal sin." Blasphemy of the Holy Spirit can only occur if a person dies having never become a follower of Christ. This is the only sin that won't be forgiven. Every other sin committed in life is atoned for by the blood of Christ, to be received by faith.

We read in 1 Corinthians 6:9-11, "Do you not know that the unrighteous will not inherit the kingdom of God? Do not be deceived: neither the sexually immoral, nor idolaters, nor adulterers, nor men who practice homosexuality, nor thieves, nor the greedy, nor drunkards, nor revilers, nor swindlers will inherit the kingdom of God. And such were some of you. But you were washed, you were sanctified, you were justified in the name of the Lord Jesus Christ and by the Spirit of our God."

Notice the sexually immoral and adulterers will be forgiven their sins if they repent of their sins and believe in the name of Christ. We read in 1 John 1:9, "If we confess our sins, he is faithful and just to forgive us our sins and cleanse us from all unrighteousness." That's all sins.

King David was a murderer and he was forgiven. In 1 Samuel 12:13, after David had an affair with Bathsheba and murdered her husband Uriah the Hittite, he told Nathan, "I have sinned against the Lord." Nathan said to him, "The Lord also has put away your sin. You shall not die." Likewise, the Apostle Paul, who was once Saul, murdered Christians, and yet he was forgiven and made an Apostle of Jesus Christ.

There is no sin that will not be forgiven except blasphemy of the Holy Spirit (and if you're reading this, you haven't committed that sin). Unlike what the Mormons teach, the spilling of your blood will not cleanse you of your sins. Only the atoning blood of Christ can make you right before God. Believe in Jesus, the God of the Bible, and you will be saved.

6) The Son is not worshiped in the same way the Father is worshiped.

In 3 Nephi 18:19, Jesus said, "Ye must always pray unto the Father in my name." It is understood by the Mormons that prayer is to God the Father and not to Jesus Christ. They interpret Exodus 20:3, "Ye shall have no other gods before me," as meaning that only God the Father receives prayer. They pray to God in the name of the Son (also Moses 5:8), but not to the Son himself. Jesus taught us to pray to the Father, and so should we.

The Mormon teachers repudiate the idea that we

should have a relationship with Jesus. Bruce McConkie said, "We worship the Father and him only and no one else. We do not worship the Son and we do not worship the Holy Ghost."[58]

From the same speech, he said "Many false and vain and foolish things are being taught in the sectarian world and even among us about our need to gain a special relationship with the Lord Jesus." He also labeled the teaching that we should have a relationship with Jesus as a false doctrine from the devil, who wants "so-called Christians to believe about Deity in order to be damned."

McConkie also appealed to the First Presidency of the Twelve and said they have never taught such a thing as to have a personal relationship with Jesus. There are many articles written and speeches given on how a Mormon can have a relationship with God. Jesus is one of those ways, but their relationship is not with Christ himself.

What the Bible Says:

In Acts 1:24, the apostles prayed specifically to Jesus that he would show them which man, between Justus and Matthias, was supposed to take Judas' place among the twelve (see also v.6). In Acts 7:59, Stephen prayed to Jesus as he was dying that the Lord would receive his spirit. The second to last

---

[58] From a speech given at Brigham Young University entitled "Our Relationship With the Lord," March 2, 1982.

verse in the Bible has John praying to Jesus that he would quickly return (Revelation 22:20).

Only those who are in Christ Jesus are able to pray prayers that are received by God. Jesus taught us that we can call upon God as our Father (Matthew 6:9) because we have received the spirit of adoption through the Son (Romans 8:15). It is because of Christ that we are called children of God, and because of him we can pray to God.

In John 14:6, Jesus said, "I am the way, and the truth, and the life. No one comes to the Father except through me." It is Christ, very God and very man, who makes access to God possible (see also John 14:13, Romans 8:34, 1 Timothy 2:5, Hebrews 7:25). The Spirit also intercedes for us (Romans 8:26-27), meaning that prayers we pray to the Spirit are also heard by God.

Jesus prayed for his disciples, as he also prayed for us, "This is eternal life: that they know you, the only true God, and Jesus Christ, whom you have sent." He was not praying for just anyone, but specifically his followers, that we would know him, meaning that we would grow in a relationship with him.

Jesus said, "I will not leave you as orphans; I will come to you" (John 14:18), and that he would be with us always, even to the end of the age (Matthew 28:20). Jesus called his disciples his brothers and sisters (Mark 3:34). He said that to care for his followers was the same as caring for him (Matthew 25:40), and to persecute his followers was the same as persecuting him (Acts 9:5). Hebrews 4:15 says that Jesus sympathizes with us in our weaknesses. Does that sound like a Savior we're not supposed to have a relationship with?

We read in 1 John 5:20, "And we know that the Son of God has come and has given us under-standing, so that we may know him who is true; and we are in him who is true, in his Son Jesus Christ. He is the true God and eternal life." Jesus is not less than God. He is the true God. Romans 9:5 says that he "is the Christ, who is God over all, blessed forever. Amen."

The Mormon teaching that "special relationship with the Lord Jesus" is "to be damned" is a horrific, Satanic doctrine that means to keep men in darkness and away from the light, who is Christ.

7) After his resurrection, Jesus Christ came to the Americas.

In John 10:16, Jesus said, "Other sheep I have, which are not of this fold: them also I must bring, and they shall hear my voice; and there shall be one fold, and one shepherd." The Mormons believe that according to 3 Nephi 16:1, Jesus was announcing he would go to the Americas and preach the gospel there. The "other sheep" were the Indians who would hear him and believe.

The Book of Mormon testifies that some of the events that occurred during Jesus' crucifixion were experienced at the same time in the Americas (introduction to 3 Nephi 8). One of those events was darkness that covered the land for three days. During that time of darkness, the voice of Jesus could be "heard among all the inhabitants of the earth" (3 Nephi 9:1, and speaking the rest of the chapter).

The next chapter begins, "And now behold, it came to pass that all the people of the land did hear these sayings, and did witness of it" (3 Nephi 10:1). And after the voice of Jesus stopped speaking, the darkness was lifted at the end of those three days, and the earth stopped trembling (v.9). It says in 11:2 that the darkness and the earthquakes were a sign that corresponded with Jesus' death.

Not long after, a voice was heard three times from heaven. On the third time, the people understood it as being God the Father, saying, "Behold my Beloved Son, in whom I am well pleased, in whom I have glorified my name—hear ye him" (c.11:7). Then they saw Jesus descending from heaven. He showed them his scars after being crucified, said he had been slain for the sins of the world, and told them to be baptized in water.

More teachings of Jesus are recorded in 3 Nephi 12-18, including the appointment of twelve apostles given the power to baptize, another version of the Sermon On the Mount, and the administration of the

Lord's supper. He also healed the sick and performed many miracles, then he ascended into heaven again. It is the most important event in the Book of Mormon, though it occupies a very small section.

What the Bible Says:

It's ironic the way Joseph Smith used John 10:16. In the context of that passage, Jesus was not talking about going to the Americas—he was warning about false teachers!

Starting in verse 10, Jesus said: "The thief comes only to steal and kill and destroy. I came that they may have life and have it abundantly. I am the good shepherd. The good shepherd lays down his life for the sheep. He who is a hired hand and not a shepherd, who does not own the sheep, sees the wolf coming and leaves the sheep and flees, and the wolf snatches them and scatters them. He flees because he is a hired hand and cares nothing for the sheep. I am the good shepherd. I know my own and my own know me, just as the Father knows me and I know the Father; and I lay down my life for the sheep. And I have other sheep that are not of this fold. I must bring them also, and they will listen to my voice. So there will be one flock, one shepherd."

Those who are truly his sheep will not follow the false teachers—they will know the voice of the Good Shepherd and follow him.

Jesus was speaking to the Jews. The "other

sheep" he told them about were the Gentiles, to whom the gospel would be taken (Acts 1:8, 9:15). The Mormons believe the Indians were descendants of Jews who had wandered over to the western world. If they were Jews, they can't be "other sheep."

We can clearly discern from Scripture that Jesus did not come to the Americas and preach to the Indians. Jesus said, "If any man say unto you, Lo, here is Christ, or there; believe it not" (Matthew 24:23). He said his next appearance would be seen by the whole world.

As given by the Apostle Paul: "For the Lord himself shall descend from heaven with a shout, with the voice of the archangel, and with the trump of God: and the dead in Christ shall rise first: Then we which are alive and remain shall be caught up together with them in the clouds, to meet the Lord in the air: and so shall we ever be with the Lord" (1 Thessalonians 4:16-17).

Forty days after Jesus' resurrection, he ascended into heaven. As the disciples were looking up, two angels appeared beside them and said, "Ye men of Galilee, why stand ye gazing up into heaven? This same Jesus, which is taken up from you into heaven, shall so come in like manner as ye have seen him go into heaven" (Acts 1:11). If Jesus came to the Americas, then he returned to earth in a manner different than what the Bible says.

As for the events that took place during Jesus'

death, darkness did not cover the earth for three days, but three hours (Matthew 27:45, Mark 15:33, Luke 23:44). An earthquake occurred in what seemed to be only a moment, not the span of three hours, and certainly not three days (Matthew 27:51). No other natural disasters are recorded.

If the voice of Jesus from heaven was heard by the whole world, there should be some evidence or written record of it somewhere in antiquity. But there is nothing—not among the Indians nor anyone else, and it's especially not in the Bible.

8) The Church of Jesus Christ of Latter-day Saints teaches a different Jesus.

In the Pearl of Great Price, Joseph Smith asked God the Father and Jesus Christ, who stood before him, which church he should join—the Presbyterians, Baptists, or Methodists. "I was answered that I must join none of them, for they were all wrong; and the Personage who addressed me said that all their creeds were an abomination in his sight; that those professors were all corrupt; that: 'they draw near to me with their lips, but their hearts are far from me, they teach for doctrines the commandments of men, having a form of godliness, but they deny the power thereof'" (Joseph Smith—History, 1:19).

In a June 20, 1998 edition of *Deseret News*, it is recorded: "In bearing testimony of Jesus Christ, [LDS President Gordon B. Hinkley] spoke of those outside the Church who say Latter-day Saints "do not believe in the traditional Christ. No, I don't. The traditional Christ of whom they speak is not the Christ of whom I speak. For the Christ of whom I speak has been revealed in this, the Dispensation of the Fullness of Times. He together with His Father appeared to the boy Joseph Smith in the year 1820, and when Joseph left the grove that day, he knew more of the nature of God than all the learned ministers of the gospel of the ages."

What the Bible Says:

In Matthew 16, Jesus asked his disciples, "Who do people say that the Son of Man is?" And they said, "Some say John the Baptist, others say Elijah, and others Jeremiah or one of the prophets." Jesus said to them, "But who do you say that I am?" And Simon Peter replied, "You are the Christ, the Son of the living God." Jesus said, "Blessed are you, Simon Bar-Jonah! For flesh and blood has not revealed this to you, but my Father who is in heaven."

It's not enough to know the name of Jesus. It is not enough to believe that Jesus was just some great prophet or did amazing things. We must believe the truth of who he is and what he did—the true Christ, the Son of the living God, as recorded in the true Scriptures.

Even the demons knew who he was (Mark 5:7). James said, "You believe that God is one; you do well. Even the demons believe—and shudder!" But the Mormons don't even believe that much. Remember, they believe that God the Father, God the Son, and God the Holy Spirit are three different gods, not the one true God.

The Apostle Paul warned that there were false teachers who would come and proclaim a different Jesus (2 Corinthians 11:4). Many Mormon teachers confess to believing in a different Christ, as Joseph Smith did. Of them, Paul said, "For such men are false apostles, deceitful workmen, disguising themselves as apostles of Christ" (v.13).

The Jesus Christ of the Latter-day Saints is one god among many gods, the first begotten son of an exalted man. He is not the creator of all things, and his atoning blood only makes forgiveness possible but not guaranteed. That is not the Jesus Christ of the Bible. If they believe in a different Jesus, they believe in a different gospel. If they believe in a different gospel, they're still dead in their sins and they are not saved.

Believe in the *right* Jesus. Repent of your sins and believe on the name of Jesus Christ—the true Christ written about in the true word of God—and you will be saved.

What the Mormons Believe About
Salvation

1) A person is saved by grace and their works.

In the Book of Mormon, 2 Nephi 25:23 reads, "For we labor diligently to write, to persuade our children, and also our brethren, to believe in Christ, and to be reconciled to God; for we know that it is by grace that we are saved, after all we can do."

Moroni 10:32 says, "If ye shall deny yourselves of all ungodliness, and love God with all your might, mind and strength, then is his grace sufficient for you, that by his grace ye may be perfect in Christ."

In Alma 11:37, it reads, "And I say unto you again that he cannot save them in their sins; for I cannot deny his word, and he hath said that no unclean thing can inherit the kingdom of heaven; therefore, how can ye be saved, except ye inherit the kingdom of heaven? Therefore, ye cannot be saved in your sins."

Doctrine and Covenants 1:32 says, "Nevertheless,

he that repents and does the commandments of the Lord shall be forgiven." In 25:15, it says, "Keep my commandments continually, and a crown of righteousness thou shalt receive. And except thou do this, where I am you cannot come." In 132:12, it says, "No man shall come unto the Father but by me or by my word, which is my law, saith the Lord."

The third article of faith reads, "We believe that through the Atonement of Christ, all mankind may be saved, by obedience to the laws and ordinances of the Gospel."

What the Bible Says:

In direct contrast with 2 Nephi 25:23, Ephesians 2:8-9 says, "For by grace are ye saved through faith; and that not of yourselves: it is the gift of God: Not of works, lest any man should boast."[59]

Furthermore, the statement in 2 Nephi 25:23, that "it is by grace that we are saved, after all we can do," is impossible. There will *always* be more that you could have done. Instead of watching a movie, you could have been praying; instead of buying a new piece of furniture, you could have been helping the poor; instead of going to the park, you could have been going door to door to sharing the gospel. If we are saved only "after all we can do," we will never be saved, because will never have done enough.

---

[59] And as we saw previously, Joseph Smith was quite the boaster regarding the things he accomplished

Praise God that's not what the Bible says. We read in Titus 3:5, "Not by works of righteousness which we have done, but according to his mercy he saved us, by the washing of regeneration, and renewing of the Holy Ghost; Which he shed on us abundantly through Jesus Christ our Saviour; That being justified by his grace, we should be made heirs according to the hope of eternal life."

Repentance is not something that a person must do first and then be saved. Rather, repentance is the evidence that one's heart has been regenerated by the Holy Spirit.

It is still the responsibility of every person—when they hear the gospel of Jesus Christ and the command to repent—to turn from their sin and follow Jesus. But we know by what the Bible says that such a response is not the work or will of man. It is the work and will of God.

We are absolutely called upon to do works. But the works that we do—including repentance, faith, baptism, partaking in the Lord's supper, loving others, and so on—are a reflection of the change that has occurred in our hearts.

Ephesians 2:10 goes on to say, "For we are his workmanship, created in Christ Jesus for good works, which God prepared beforehand, that we should walk in them." This comes after Paul said we are not saved by works (v.8-9). So our works are the outward expression of an inward change. They do not save us. They're the evidence that we are saved. Obedience and faith are the fruit of the righteousness of Christ, given by God.

Romans 3:21-25 reads, "But now the righteousness of God has been manifested apart from the law, although the Law and the Prophets bear witness to it—the righteousness of God through faith in Jesus Christ for all who believe. For there is no distinction: for all have sinned and fall short of the glory of God, and are justified by his grace as a gift, through the redemption that is in Christ Jesus, whom God put forward as a propitiation by his blood, to be received by faith."

In Galatians 3:5, Paul says, "Does he who supplies the Spirit to you and works miracles among you do so by works of the law, or by hearing with faith?" In other words, are you saved by works of the law, or are you saved by faith? It has to be one or the other. It cannot be both. It is by grace we are saved through faith.

Galatians 5:4 says, "You are severed from Christ, you who would be justified by the law; you have fallen away from grace." If you try to be saved by works of the law, you are severed from Christ and you are not saved. Romans 3:28 puts it plainly: "Therefore we conclude that a man is justified by faith without the deeds of the law."

The law is powerless to save (Romans 8:3-4, Hebrews 7:19, 10:1), so obedience cannot save. Only

Christ saves us, by himself, by grace alone through faith alone. That's the gospel truth.

2) The basic requirements for salvation are faith, repentance, baptism, and confirmation.

The fourth article of faith is, "We believe that the first principles and ordinances of the Gospel are: first, Faith in the Lord Jesus Christ; second, Repentance; third, Baptism by immersion for the remission of sins; fourth, Laying on of hands for the gift of the Holy Ghost."

According to the *Gospel Doctrine Teacher's Manual*, the kind of faith one must have is specifically in the restored gospel as it was given to Joseph Smith by the angel Moroni.[60]

What the Bible Says:

As mentioned in Ephesians 2:8, faith is given by God: "For by grace are ye saved through faith; and that not of yourselves: it is the gift of God." Grace, salvation, and faith are all gifts from God. Hebrews 12:2 says that Jesus is the "author and finisher of our faith." He gave us our faith, and he is perfecting our faith.

When the Bible says that Jesus is the author of faith, it means more than him being the author of a religious belief. He's the author of the very *ability* to

---

[60] Doctrine and Covenants and Church History: Gospel Doctrine Teacher's Manual, 1999, pg. 35-40.

believe. John 6:29 says, "This is the work of God, that you believe in him whom he has sent." Romans 12:3 says that God apportions the measure of faith that we have. Faith and belief are the work of God, not man.

Repentance itself is also the work of God. It says in 2 Timothy 2:25 that God is the one who grants repentance. Likewise in Acts 5:31, "God exalted him at his right hand as Leader and Savior, to give repentance to Israel and forgiveness of sins." And in Acts 11:18, "When they heard these things they fell silent. And they glorified God, saying, 'Then to the Gentiles also God has granted repentance that leads to life."

Faith is indeed necessary for salvation, but not the kind of faith the Mormon church says one must have. The Mormon faith is no faith at all, for it is to believe Joseph Smith's teaching in a different god and a different Jesus than the God of the Bible.

3) One must be baptized — and be baptized in the Mormon church — in order to be saved.

In the King Follett Discourse, Smith said, "Many talk of baptism not being essential to salvation; but this kind of teaching would lay the foundation of their damnation. I have the truth, and am at the defiance of the world to contradict me, if they can."

While Smith was translating the Book of Mormon, he read passages about baptism for salvation.

On May 15, 1829, he and his scribe Oliver Cowdry went into the woods to ask God about baptism. It is recounted that as they prayed, John the Baptist descended from heaven, laid his hands on them, and gave them the Aaronic Priesthood (which had vanished from the earth during the Great Apostasy). Smith and Cowdry were then able to baptize one another.[61]

The offices of the Aaronic Priesthood are bishop, priest, teacher, and deacon, and any of them may administer baptism under the authority of the presiding priesthood leader. The Aaronic priesthood is subject to the Melchizedek priesthood which a person in the Aaronic priesthood can aspire to attain.

According to Mormon.org, "Jesus Christ taught that baptism is essential to the salvation of all who have lived on earth (see John 3:5)."[62] A person must be baptized by the proper authority, which was granted to Joseph Smith by John the Baptist, and the apostles Peter, James, and John to Joseph Smith. No other church has the proper authority (Doctrine and Covenants 132:7, 13).[63]

---

[61] Joseph Smith—History 1:68-72. According to an LDS historical document dated December 18, 1833, found in the Patriarchal Blessing Book 1, pg 8-9, John the Baptist is an angel.

[62] https://www.mormon.org/faq/topic/baptism

[63] Joseph Smith was also visited by Moses, Elijah, and other Bible figures. According to Doctrines and Covenants 7:1-3, the Apostle John is still alive, roaming this earth until the Lord's return. If this is so, why hasn't he shown up to affirm Mormonism or take his rightful place among the Quorum of the Twelve Apostles?

What the Bible Says:

In Acts 10, the Apostle Peter was invited to the house of Cornelius to preach. After sharing the gospel, the Holy Spirit came upon all who heard it. Then Peter said, "Can anyone withhold water for baptizing these people, who have received the Holy Spirit just as we have?" And he commanded them to be baptized in the name of Jesus Christ (v.47-48).

Note that they received the Holy Spirit first, *and then* they were baptized.[64] They were saved before they had received their baptism. Water baptism is an outward expression of an inward change. Water does not have salvific properties. No one is saved by being baptized in water, no matter who does the baptizing.

Jesus Christ did teach that baptism was essential for salvation—not *water* baptism, but baptism of the Holy Spirit. In John 3:5, Jesus said, "Truly, truly, I say to you, unless one is born of water and the Spirit, he cannot enter the kingdom of God." Many false teachers—in addition to Joseph Smith—have twisted this verse as meaning a person must be baptized in water in order to be saved.

Jesus was talking to Nicodemus, a Pharisee, and in much of what Jesus said, he was explaining what had already been written by the prophets. Being born

---

[64] A Mormon would argue that their baptism *sealed* the Holy Spirit. They would have had the Spirit for only a time. He would not have remained if they had not been baptized. But the Spirit is the one who does the sealing, not the person (see Ephesians 1:13 and 4:30).

of water and the Spirit was a reference to something that had been written by the prophet Ezekiel. Nicodemus should have known of what Jesus was speaking because Nicodemus was a teacher in Israel.[65] Jesus said to him, "Are you the teacher of Israel and yet you do not understand these things?" (John 3:10)

In Ezekiel 36:25-27, we read, "I will sprinkle clean water on you, and you shall be clean from all your uncleannesses, and from all your idols I will cleanse you. And I will give you a new heart, and a new spirit I will put within you. And I will remove the heart of stone from your flesh and give you a heart of flesh. And I will put my Spirit within you, and cause you to walk in my statutes and be careful to obey my rules."

Clearly, Ezekiel's reference is not to the element of water, and neither was that Jesus' reference. He was talking about being cleansed by God.

As quoted earlier, Titus 3:5 says, "He saved us, not because of works done by us in righteousness, but according to his own mercy, by the washing of regeneration and renewal of the Holy Spirit." In Ephesians 5:25-26, we read, "Husbands, love your wives, as Christ loved the church and gave himself up for her, that he might sanctify her, having cleansed her by the washing of water with the word."

---

[65] Likewise, if Joseph Smith really was a prophet of God, he would have known what Jesus was talking about.

In 1 Corinthians 6:9-11, we read, "Do you not know that the unrighteous will not inherit the kingdom of God? Do not be deceived: neither the sexually immoral, nor idolaters, nor adulterers, nor men who practice homosexuality, nor thieves, nor the greedy, nor drunkards, nor revilers, nor swindlers will inherit the kingdom of God. And such were some of you. But you were washed, you were sanctified, you were justified in the name of the Lord Jesus Christ and by the Spirit of our God."

In none of these three aforementioned passages would we attribute *water* or being *washed* to physical water. This is clearly a metaphorical reference to a spiritual cleansing. Such is the case also with John 3:5.

In 1 Peter 3:21, Peter says, "Baptism, which corresponds to this, now saves you, not as a removal of dirt from the body but as an appeal to God for a good conscience, through the resurrection of Jesus Christ." Water baptism *corresponds* to our spiritual cleansing, but doesn't actually cleanse us.

Note that it is "an appeal to God for a good conscience," not an appeal for salvation. We are displaying on the outside what has happened on the inside, and in the forgiveness that we've already been given, we are appealing that our conscience likewise be cleansed, no longer burdened by the guilt of past sins, knowing in our minds that we have been made a new creature in Christ Jesus.

Concerning this reinstatement of priesthoods, the Aaronic priesthood didn't disappear in some Great Apostasy. It was fulfilled at the cross. Hebrews 4:14-16 says, "Since then we have a great high priest who has passed through the heavens, Jesus, the Son of God, let us hold fast our confession. For we do not have a high priest who is unable to sympathize with our weaknesses, but one who in every respect has been tempted as we are, yet without sin. Let us then with confidence draw near to the throne of grace, that we may receive mercy and find grace to help in time of need." [66]

The book of Hebrews speaks extensively about this. There is no earthly priesthood, for Jesus alone holds the Melchizedek priesthood (Hebrews 5:6).

4) There are three levels of heaven one can reach depending on their works.

In February 1832, Joseph Smith was translating the gospel of John. He said, "It appeared self-evident from what truths were left, that if God rewarded every one according to the deeds done in the body, the term 'Heaven,' as intended for the Saints' eternal

---

[66] The Book of Mormon talks about worship and sacrifices conducted in Hebrew temples in the Americas prior to Jesus' appearance. This is also a contradiction of Scripture, for God had chosen the place of the temple, and that place was Mount Moriah in Jerusalem (1 Kings 11:36, 2 Chronicles 3:1). There was only one temple because there is only one God. Then again, Mormons believe in many gods, so they believe in many temples.

home, must include more kingdoms than one."

In the home of John Johnson in Hiram, OH, Smith "saw a vision of the three degrees of glory that God has prepared for his children. The Prophet translated John 5:29, which describes how all 'shall come forth' in the resurrection — 'they that have done good, unto the resurrection of life; and they that have done evil, unto the resurrection of damnation.'"

He claimed that John 14:2, where Jesus said, "In my Father's house are many *mansions*," should actually be read, "In my Father's house are many *kingdoms*." He said, "There are mansions for those who obey a celestial law, and there are other mansions for those who come short of the law, every man in his own order."

Smith also said that Paul mentions three different levels of heaven in 1 Corinthians 15:40-41, and in 2 Corinthians 12:2-4 where Paul talks about knowing "a man that was caught up to the third heaven." The three levels of heaven that Smith saw were called the Telestial, Terrestrial, and Celestial levels.

The celestial is the highest and it is attained by those who believe in Jesus Christ as Joseph Smith spoke of him, repent of their sins, are baptized in water (which can only be done by someone in the Aaronic priesthood), and receive the Holy Ghost by the laying on of hands (which can only be done by someone in the Melchizedek priesthood). They must also show their worthiness by obedience to the gospel rules and principles.

The middle level of heaven is the terrestrial kingdom, attained by those who did not know the law of God in life, but the Son preached it to them after death and they believed. Said Smith, "These are they who are honorable men of the earth, who were blinded by the craftiness of men. These are they who receive of his glory, but not of his fullness. They are they who receive of the presence of the Son, but not of the fullness of the Father. Wherefore, they are bodies terrestrial, and not bodies celestial, and differ in glory as the moon differs from the sun."

The lower level of heaven is the telestial kingdom.[67] According to Smith, those in the telestial realm "are they who received not the gospel of Christ, neither the testimony of Jesus. These are they who deny not the Holy Spirit. These are they who are thrust down to hell. These are they who shall not be redeemed from the devil until the last resurrection, until the Lord, even Christ the Lamb, shall have finished his work."[68]

Those who were Mormon and faithfully kept all the gospel rules and principles before they died will go to paradise awaiting the final judgment when they will then gain access to the celestial kingdom.

[67] Joseph Smith coined the word "telestial" by combining the words celestial and terrestrial.

[68] Teachings of the Presidents of the Church: Joseph Smith, 2011, pg. 217-226. The heavenly vision presumably given to Joseph Smith and Signey Rigdon is also in Doctrine and Covenants, 76.

Those who die and were not Mormon will go to what is called the spirit prison. But even from the spirit prison, it is possible for a person to get to the celestial kingdom according to their actions after they have died. [69]

What the Bible Says:

In John 5:25-29, Jesus said, "Truly, truly, I say to you, an hour is coming, and is now here, when the dead will hear the voice of the Son of God, and those who hear will live. For as the Father has life in himself, so he has granted the Son to have life in himself. And he has given him authority to execute judgment, because he is the Son of Man. Do not marvel at this, for an hour is coming when all who are in the tombs will hear his voice and come out, those who have done good to the resurrection of life, and those who have done evil to the resurrection of judgment."

Joseph Smith took this passage to mean that Jesus would witness to the dead in a spiritual prison[70] and they would believe and enter into another "level" of heaven, the terrestrial kingdom according to his vision. But that wasn't what Jesus was talking about.

Jesus was saying that even at that very moment ("an hour is coming, and *is now here*") his words

---

[69] The telestial kingdom is still regarded as being remarkable. Presumably Joseph Smith said that if you were to catch a glimpse of the telestial kingdom, you'd commit suicide just to get there.

[70] Based also on misunderstanding 1 Peter 3:19.

would minister to those who were dead—meaning, dead in their sins. That can't mean that he was going into spiritual prisons and ministering to dead people because, at that very moment, he was standing right in front of them.

Ephesians 2:1 says that we are dead in our trespasses and sins, and verse 5 says we are made alive with Christ. Remember, because of sin, we're born physically alive but spiritually dead. It is by hearing the gospel and believing in Jesus that a person is brought from death to life. Romans 10:17 says that faith comes from hearing, and hearing through the word of Christ.

Joseph Smith simply didn't understand what this meant. He was writing his own version of the gospel of John, and when he came to chapter 5, he got this idea of multiple levels of heaven, which he claimed was a vision from the Lord.

In 1 Corinthians 15:35-49, Paul was saying very simply that our physical bodies are perishable and cannot inherit eternal life. They must be changed by the one who has the power to change them. As Paul put it to the Philippians, God will "transform our lowly body to be like his glorious body, by the power that enables him even to subject all things to himself" (Philippians 3:21).

In 1 Corinthians 15, starting in verse 40, Paul wrote, "There are heavenly bodies and earthly bodies, but the glory of the heavenly is of one kind, and the glory of the earthly is another. There is one glory of the sun, and another glory of the moon, and another glory of the stars; for star differs from star in glory. So is it with the resurrection of the dead. What is sown is perishable; what is raised is imperishable. It is sown in dishonor; it is raised in glory. It is sown in weakness; it is raised in power. It is sown a natural body; it is raised a spiritual body. If there is a natural body, there is also a spiritual body."

When Paul referenced the earthly, the sun, moon, and stars, he wasn't talking about the earth and three levels of heaven. When you look at the mountains, a glorious *earthly* creation, are you not awed by their beauty? When you look at the sun, it is beautiful in its own way, but it is not like the mountains. Likewise, the moon is beautiful in its own way, but it's not like the sun. The entire cosmos of the stars have a splendor all their own as well.

Well, just as God is able to give a unique splendor to things that are physical, so he is able to do with things that are not physical. It is a blessed hope and an assurance to us that he is able to take a sinful, dishonorable, perishable, dead body and make it into a perfect, honorable, imperishable, living body that is fit for his kingdom, which we cannot inhabit in our current bodies.

Paul also used the analogy of a seed. Just as a seed falls to the ground and dies and grows into a new life, a flowering plant, so it is the same with the body—it falls to the ground and it dies, and God raises up from that a new and even more glorious life. This is the promise for all those who are in Christ Jesus.

Smith's other reference was 2 Corinthians 12:2-3 where Paul says, "I know a man in Christ who fourteen years ago was caught up to the third heaven—whether in the body or out of the body I do not know, God knows. And I know that this man was caught up into paradise—whether in the body or out of the body I do not know, God knows."

This third heaven is not supposed to be some crude description of a multi-tiered heaven. It's a common-sense distinction between the sky where the birds and clouds are (the first heaven); the sky inhabited by the sun, moon, and stars (the second heaven); and the spiritual realm where God dwells (the third heaven).

By the way, this man that Paul said he knew who was caught up to heaven? He was talking about himself. He was so humbled by his experience that he couldn't use personal pronouns. Instead, he described the experience in the third person. He said nothing about what he saw: "he heard things that cannot be told, which man may not utter" (v.4). That's it. That's all we get about Paul's experience regarding heaven.

Contrast that with Joseph Smith's experience and the pride by which he continually boasted about himself.[71]

In the whole Bible, only four men had a vision of heaven: Isaiah, Ezekiel, Paul, and John. Only three of those four men wrote about what they saw, and the details that they gave about heaven were sparse. What they were fixated on wasn't heaven—it was the glory of God! They were overwhelmed, petrified, awe-struck, dumb-founded, silenced, and fell on their faces in fear and in worship.

That wasn't Joseph Smith's response to seeing God in his heaven. God himself seemed to be the least interesting thing to Smith and Rigdon, who shared the vision with Smith. What they were most interested in was the things that suited man, not God in all his glory.

A man named Philo Dibble was also in the home when Smith and Rigdon received their vision of heaven, and he wrote about what he observed in their mannerisms. He said, "Joseph sat firmly and calmly at the time, in the midst of a magnificent glory, but Sidney sat limp and pale, apparently as limp as a rag. Observing such at the close of the vision, Joseph remarked smilingly, 'Sidney is not as used to it as I am.'"[72]

---

[71] The King Follett Discourse is very prideful. One wouldn't need to go farther than that for an example as to see how full of himself Joseph Smith really was.

[72] The Kingdom of God Restored, pg. 156-157, as recounted in Primary 5: Doctrine and Covenants and Church History, 1997, pg. 121-126.

Even Rigdon's more *humbled* reaction was no where near the way the prophets and the apostles responded to seeing visions of heaven.[73]

5) Hell is reserved for apostate Mormons, and the devil and his demons.

In Doctrine and Covenants 76:30-38, in his vision of heaven, Joseph Smith also saw what would happen to those who had once been partakers with the Church of Jesus Christ of Latter-day Saints but then left the faith:

"They are they who are the sons of perdition, of whom I say that it had been better for them never to have been born; For they are vessels of wrath, doomed to suffer the wrath of God, with the devil and his angels in eternity; Concerning whom I have said there is no forgiveness in this world nor in the world to come—Having denied the Holy Spirit after having received it, and having denied the Only Begotten Son of the Father, having crucified him unto themselves and put him to an open shame. These are they who shall go away into the lake of fire and

---

[73] Rigdon was not a witness to a vision—he was in on it. The receiving of the vision involved Smith and Rigdon acting like they were in a trance-like state. Rigdon would say, "What do I see?" Then Smith would explain it to him, and Rigdon would say, "I see the same." Then Smith would say, "What do I see?" and Rigdon would explain it to him, and Smith would say, "I see the same." It made it seem like two men were witnessing the same vision, but it was a ruse. Some apostolic teachers today will use the same trickery.

brimstone with the devil and his angels—And the only ones on whom the second death shall have any power; Yea, verily, the only ones who shall not be redeemed in the due time of the Lord, after the sufferings of his wrath."

Anyone who had been baptized to receive the Holy Ghost but then denied the Mormon faith committed an unforgivable sin and were consigned to eternal purgatory. People like Hitler, Stalin, Margaret Sanger, Jeffery Dahmer—these would go to the Telestial kingdom, not hell. Apostate Mormons are considered the worst of the worst, according to Smith.[74]

He said the following in the King Follett Discourse: "All sins shall be forgiven, except the sin against the Holy Ghost; for Jesus will save all except the sons of perdition. What must a man do to commit the un-pardonable sin? He must receive the Holy Ghost, have the heavens opened unto him, and know God, and then sin against him. After a man has sinned against the Holy Ghost, there is no repentance for him… This is the case with many apostates of the Church of Jesus Christ of Latter-day Saints."

---

[74] Even in hell, apostate Mormons would still reign over the devil and his angels, because they had mortal bodies and got further in the process of the Law of Eternal Progression than the demons did. There's still a consolation prize, even for an apostate.

What the Bible Says:

Jesus does talk about an unforgivable sin—blasphemy of the Holy Spirit—in Matthew 12, Mark 3, and in Luke 12. In Luke 12:10, he says, "And everyone who speaks a word against the Son of Man will be forgiven, but the one who blasphemes against the Holy Spirit will not be forgiven."

In other words, blasphemy against God or Jesus is hastily spoken and God extends such grace to us that we will be forgiven of this sin. If we ask him for forgiveness, he will cleanse us from all unrighteousness (John 14:13-14, 1 John 1:9).

But if a person persistently refuses the message of the Holy Spirit, who testifies about Christ as the Son of God (1 John 5:6), and if they reject the message of the gospel all the way to their death, that is a willful, unrepentant, conscious rejection of God. That will not be forgiven. That describes every person who dies not having believed in Jesus as Lord. They are guilty of blasphemy of the Holy Spirit.

If a person is asking now if they've committed the unforgivable sin, they haven't, for the conviction in their hearts is evidence that they are open to the work of the Spirit (John 16:8-11). We should regard no one this side of heaven has having committed the unforgivable sin. Everyone must be told the gospel of Jesus Christ, and they can be saved.

The Bible is clear who goes to hell: "But as for the cowardly, the faithless, the detestable, as for murderers, the sexually immoral, sorcerers, idolaters, and all liars, their portion will be in the lake that burns with fire and sulfur, which is the second death" (Revelation 21:8).

No one goes to hell for being an apostate Mormon. They go to hell because they did not worship the one true God and his true Son, Jesus Christ. Joseph Smith's doctrine regarding apostate Mormons is mere fear-mongering. In order to retain a large number of followers and hinder a person from listening to — well — resources such as this one, Smith had built into his religion the worst of penalties for those who leave Mormonism.

The true believer knows that what he deserves is the judgement and wrath of God. But because God is loving and merciful, what he has received is God's forgiveness and grace through the sacrifice of Christ. Everyone deserves to go to hell. It is the people whom Christ has redeemed from all lawlessness and purified for his own possession (Titus 2:14) that are fellow heirs to his eternal and perfect kingdom.

6) A person can still be saved even after they die.

In the King Follett Discourse, Smith said, "If a man has knowledge, he can be saved; although, if he has been guilty of great sins, he will be punished for them. But when he consents to obey the gospel, whether here or in the world of spirits, he is saved."

Even after death, a person still has an opportunity to believe in the Mormon faith, repent of their sins, and receive the Holy Ghost. However, it is not possible for a spirit to be baptized in water. They need someone to be baptized for them in life in order to fulfill that requirement. This is the practice of baptism of the dead.

In Doctrine and Covenants 127:5-7, Smith wrote, "Verily, thus saith the Lord unto you concerning your dead: When any of you are baptized for your dead, let there be a recorder, and let him be eyewitness of your baptisms; let him hear with his ears, that he may testify of a truth, saith the Lord; That in all your recordings it may be recorded in heaven; whatsoever you bind on earth, may be bound in heaven; whatsoever you loose on earth, may be loosed in heaven; For I am about to restore many things to the earth, pertaining to the priesthood, saith the Lord of Hosts."

In 128:5, Smith said that this baptism was "for the salvation of the dead who should die without a knowledge of the gospel" and that "the nature of this ordinance consists in the power of the priesthood" (v.8). A living person is baptized for a dead person because they are the likeness of that person. Their baptism represents "the dead in coming forth out of their graves" (v.12). The pool, also called a baptismal font, represents a grave, and is supposed to be constructed beneath ground-level (v.13).

A Mormon will go to the Mormon temple and

have a list of names of those who are dead, and will be baptized on their behalf.[75] A spirit who is in the spirit prison cannot be baptized in water for they are spirit, so a living person must be baptized for them. This fulfills one of the gospel requirements for a person to be saved so that they may enter one of the levels of heaven.[76]

According to Joseph Fielding Smith, the prophet Smith said, "The greatest responsibility in this world that God has laid upon us is to seek after our dead."[77]

What the Bible Says:

In Luke 16:19-31, Jesus told a story about an unnamed rich man and a poor man named Lazarus. The rich man enjoyed abundance while Lazarus suffered and eventually died, carried by angels to Abraham's side. The rich man also died, but he went to a place of torment.

From there he could see Lazarus with Abraham and begged for relief: "Father Abraham, have mercy

---

[75] Many of the popular family tree and ancestry websites, such as Ancestry.com, are owned by the Mormon church. They have access to everyone's lineage so that they may conduct their baptisms for the dead.

[76] Even after death, missionary work doesn't end for the Mormon. Missionaries will leave paradise and minister to the spirits in the spirit prison so they would hear the teachings of Joseph Smith, repent of their sins, and receive the Holy Spirit. If they've also had someone baptized for them, it's possible for them to enter even the celestial kingdom.

[77] The Teachings of the Prophet Joseph Smith, pg. 356.

on me, and send Lazarus to dip the end of his finger in water and cool my tongue, for I am in anguish in this flame!"

Abraham replied, "Child, remember that you in your lifetime received your good things, and Lazarus in like manner bad things; but now he is comforted here, and you are in anguish. And besides all this, between us and you a great chasm has been fixed, in order that those who would pass from here to you may not be able, and none may cross from there to us." (Clearly the dead cannot be delivered from their sentence.)

The rich man also asked that he be able to go back and warn his brothers so they would not end up in such an awful place. Abraham replied, "They have Moses and the Prophets. Let them hear them."

The rich man said, "No, father Abraham, but if someone goes to them from the dead, they will repent!"

Abraham said, "If they do not hear Moses and the Prophets, neither will they be convinced if someone should rise from the dead."

Hebrews 9:27 says that it is appointed for a man once to die and after that comes judgment. We have this life only to hear and respond to the gospel. There is no opportunity to repent and believe after death.

Even the Book of Mormon says that a person cannot be saved after they die! In 2 Nephi 28:8-9, it reads, "And there shall also be many which shall say:

Eat, drink, and be merry; nevertheless, fear God—he will justify in committing a little sin; yea, lie a little, take the advantage of one because of his words, dig a pit for thy neighbor; there is no harm in this; and do all these things, for tomorrow we die; and if it so be that we are guilty, God will beat us with a few stripes, and at last we shall be saved in the kingdom of God. Yea, and there shall be many which shall teach after this manner, false and vain and foolish doctrines, and shall be puffed up in their hearts, and shall seek deep to hide their counsels from the Lord; and their works shall be in the dark."

So even according to the Book of Mormon, it is "false and vain and foolish doctrines" to teach that one will be saved after death. This is one of the evidences of Mormonism's inconsistency, and how it is a religion that has evolved over time. The Book of Mormon was published in 1830. Joseph Smith introduced the doctrine of baptism for the dead over ten years later.

7) A person must be married to attain the highest level of glory.

According to Doctrine and Covenants 131:1-4, Joseph Smith said, "In the celestial glory there are three heavens or degrees; And in order to obtain the highest, a man must enter into this order of the priesthood [meaning the new and everlasting covenant of marriage]; And if he does not, he cannot obtain it. He may enter into the other, but that is the end of his kingdom; he cannot have an increase."

According to Latter-day Saint leader Milton R. Hunter, "The principal purpose of the gospel of Jesus Christ and the ultimate goal of eternal progression is to receive eternal life, i.e., to become as God is. It is thoroughly understood, however, that a vast majority of the human family will never become gods, because to do so they must accept the true gospel, receive all of the ordinances—including celestial marriage—and obey all of God's command-ments faithfully to the end."[78]

According to the LDS student manual *The Achieving of Celestial Marriage*, "God was once a man who by obedience advanced to his present state of perfection. Through obedience and celestial mar-riage, we may progress to the point where we become like Gods."[79]

The Mormon faith teaches a doctrine of not simply eternal life but eternal *lives.* Doctrine and Covenants 132:24 says, "This is eternal *lives*—to know the only wise and true God, and Jesus Christ, whom he hath sent" (emphasis added).

According to the Mormon Encyclopedia, "Eternal lives is a term that refers to the right and power to beget children after the resurrection, granted to those

[78] Christ in Ancient America, pg. 168.
[79] 1992 edition, pg. 4, courtesy of Dr. James White, Alpha and Omega Ministries.

who are exalted in the highest degree of the celestial kingdom. This is an aspect of eternal progression" (1992, pg. 465).

Joseph Smith taught, "Except a man and his wife enter into an everlasting covenant and be married for eternity, while in this probation, by the power and authority of the Holy Priesthood, they will cease to increase when they die; that is, they will not have any children after the resurrection."[80]

If a person has not been married, then when they die, they become an angel because the angels did not abide God's new and everlasting covenant which required marriage (Doctrine and Covenants 132:16-17). God, men, and angels, according to the Mormon faith, are all the same species but have reached different levels of progression.

What the Bible Says:

Romans 7:1-2 says, "Or do you not know, brothers—for I am speaking to those who know the law—that the law is binding on a person only as long as he lives? For a married woman is bound by law to her husband while he lives, but if her husband dies she is released from the law of marriage."

In Matthew 22:23-33, some Sadducees came to Jesus and said, "Teacher, Moses said, 'If a man dies having no children, his brother must marry the widow and raise up offspring for his brother.' Now

---

[80] Teachings of the Prophet Joseph Smith, pg. 300-301.

there were seven brothers among us. The first married and died, and having no offspring left his wife to his brother. So too the second and third, down to the seventh. After them all, the woman died. In the resurrection, therefore, of the seven, whose wife will she be? For they all had her."

Jesus responded to them, "You are wrong, because you know neither the Scriptures nor the power of God. For in the resurrection they neither marry nor are given in marriage, but are like angels in heaven."

In other words, in heaven she is married to no one. The Sadducees, not understanding the Scriptures, presupposed with their question that marriage was an eternal covenant. Rather, it is a temporal covenant between a man and a woman for life, "Til *death* do us part." Jesus mentioned angels because they are beings that do not reproduce, nor do they get married. So will everyone be like this in heaven.

The only marriage in heaven is between Christ and his church. In Revelation 19:7-8, we read, "Let us rejoice and exult and give him the glory, for the marriage of the Lamb has come, and his Bride has made herself ready; it was granted her to clothe herself with fine linen, bright and pure." Then in Revelation 21:2, John saw the purified church "prepared as a bride adorned for her husband."

Marriage between a man and a woman and the having of children is a picture of the relationship between Christ and his church. Paul demonstrates this in Ephesians 5:22-33 when he tells husbands to love their wives as Christ loved the church. "This mystery is profound," he says, "and I am saying that it refers to Christ and the church." In heaven we will not need such a picture anymore for we will see perfectly the church and Christ together.

John 17:3 says, "And this is eternal life," not *lives*, "that they know you the only true God, and Jesus Christ whom you have sent."

8) Jesus is not the only Savior, and you can be saviors yourselves.

In the King Follett Discourse, Joseph Smith said, "God hath made a provision that every spirit in the eternal world can be ferreted out and saved unless he has committed that unpardonable sin which cannot be remitted to him either in this world or the world of spirits. God has wrought out a salvation for all men, unless they have committed a certain sin; and every man who has a friend in the eternal world can save him, unless he has committed the unpardonable sin. And so you can see how far you can be a savior."

Remember that Mormons believe there are other worlds created and inhabited by other gods. In light of that doctrine, Brigham Young said, "Consequently every earth has its redeemer, and every earth has its tempter."[81]

---

[81] Journal of Discourses, vol. 14, pg. 71.

What the Bible Says:

Again in Isaiah 43:10-11, God says, "Before me no god was formed, nor shall there be any after me. I, I am the Lord, and besides me there is no savior."

What the Mormons Believe About
Right Living

1) The point of human existence is to learn.

In the King Follett Discourse, Joseph Smith said, "Here, then, is eternal life — to know the only wise and true God; and you have got to learn to be gods yourselves." In that sermon, he also said, "The mind or the intelligence which man possesses is co-equal with God himself."[82]

According to the Mormon law of eternal progression, the only eternal things are intelligences and matter.[83] Not even God is eternal. If God obeyed the law to become God, then the law existed before God. So we are always in a state of learning — in our pre-mortal state, during this mortal life, and after-life as well.

---

[82] In that sermon, *learn* or *learning* is mentioned up to 21 times.

[83] Yes, even God, the angels, and heaven are made of matter, according to the Mormons, but it is such a refined matter that it cannot be observed with the physical eye.

As recorded in the teachings of Brigham Young, "What are we here for? To learn to enjoy more, and to increase in knowledge and in experience. The object of this existence is to learn, which we can only do a little at a time. The whole mortal existence of man is neither more nor less than a preparatory state given to finite beings, a space wherein they may improve themselves for a higher state of being.[84]

What the Bible Says:

We read in 1 Corinthians 10:31, "Whether therefore ye eat, or drink, or whatsoever ye do, do all to the glory of God." In Revelation 4:11, "Thou art worthy, O Lord, to receive glory and honor and power: for thou hast created all things, and for thy pleasure they are and were created."

In Psalm 73:24-26, "Thou shalt guide me with thy counsel, and afterward receive me to glory. Whom have I in heaven but thee? And there is none upon earth that I desire beside thee. My flesh and my heart faileth: but God is the strength of my heart, and my portion forever."

As we read in 1 Corinthians 8:1, "knowledge puffs up, but love builds up." This puffing up with knowledges is readily displayed in the King Follett Discourse. According to Smith, a person is to learn nothing more than how to make himself better. All

---

[84] Teachings of Presidents of the Church: Brigham Young, (1997), pg. 85-86.

calls in the Mormon faith to "love" are at their root selfishly motivated for it is all to benefit the self in the end.

It is indeed fitting for us to learn, and we are commanded to study even the Scriptures (Joshua 1:8, Proverbs 4:5, 18:5, 2 Timothy 3:14-17). Those without knowledge are called fools (Psalm 82:5, 92:6, Proverbs 12:1, 15:4). But what we learn is not to benefit ourselves. It is to glorify God and worship him all the more.

In contrast with Brigham Young's teaching, the Westminster Shorter Catechism sums up the meaning of these Scriptures quite nicely with its first question: "What is the chief end of man?" Answer: "Man's chief end is to glorify God, and to enjoy him forever."

Have you noticed yet how material everything is in Mormonism? Yes, they teach about the physical and the spiritual, but the spiritual is exactly the same as the natural, but more refined. Well, the Bible has a response to that, too.

In 1 Corinthians 2:12-16, the Apostle Paul says, "Now we have received not the spirit of the world, but the Spirit who is from God, that we might understand the things freely given us by God. And we impart this in words not taught by human wisdom but taught by the Spirit, interpreting spiritual truths to those who are spiritual. The natural person does not accept the things of the Spirit of God, for they are folly to him, and he is not able to understand them because they are spiritually discerned. The spiritual person judges all things, but is himself to be judged by no one. 'For who has understood the mind of the Lord so as to instruct him?' But we have the mind of Christ."

So why didn't Joseph Smith and why don't his followers understand the truths of the Bible? Because they do not have the Spirit of God. They try to understand spiritual things in natural terms, which cannot be done.

2) Little children are incapable of sinning.

In Doctrine and Covenants 29:46-49, it says, "But behold, I say unto you, that little children are redeemed from the foundation of the world through mine Only Begotten; Wherefore, they cannot sin, for power is not given unto Satan to tempt little children, until they begin to become accountable before me; For it is given unto them even as I will, according to mine own pleasure, that great things may be required at the hand of their fathers. And, again, I say unto you, that whoso having knowledge, have I not commanded you to repent?"

According to Doctrine and Covenants 68:25, the age of accountability for a child is eight years old. Before that, a child is free from guilt, and "the sin be upon the heads of the parents."

What the Bible Says:

Romans 3:10 says, "As it is written: 'None is righteous, no, not one.'" Romans 3:23 says, "For all have sinned and fall short of the glory of God." Genesis 8:21 says that "the intention of man's heart is evil from his youth." Psalm 51:5 says, "Behold I was brought forth in iniquity, and in sin did my mother conceive me."

This might seem like a small issue, but it's actually very important. The Bible says we are born with a sin nature, a propensity to do what is selfish and evil, in rebellion against God. That is our desire from birth. God did give us a conscience—an inherent sense of moral order (Romans 2:14)—but the conscience isn't perfect. Because of the conscience, a person may not be as bad as they could be, but sinless they are not.

All children do selfish and wrong things without knowing that what they are doing is wrong. They, like all people, must be taught the difference between wrong and right. This is where the law of God comes in. The law stops a person's mouth from proclaiming their own goodness (Romans 3:19) and makes them aware of their own sin (Romans 3:20). By the law we realize that we are fallen and in need of God's grace.

When we hear from God's law commandments such as "Do not lie," "Do not steal," "Do not commit adultery," "Do not covet," we become aware that we do those things and have broken God's law even before we knew what God's law was.

Should a person boast in their self-righteousness and say, "Well, I've never had an affair, so I've never committed adultery!" Jesus said that even if you look at a woman with lust in your heart, you've committed adultery with her in your heart (Matthew 5:28).

Should a person say, "Well, I've never committed murder before, so I'm innocent of that sin!" Jesus said that if you've ever had contempt for another person and called them names, you have murdered that person in your heart and will be subject to the fires of hell (Matthew 5:22).

Therefore, our sin is not a matter of what we do on the outside. It comes from inside — a corrupt heart that has been in rebellion against God from birth. Once we've been presented with the law of God and shown our sinful nature, our heart is then open to receive the message of God's saving grace in the gospel of Jesus Christ.

Romans 3:23 goes on, "For all have sinned and fall short of the glory of God; and are justified by his grace as a gift, through the redemption that is in Christ Jesus, whom God put forward as a propitiation by his blood, to be received by faith."

If learning is the point of human existence, as the Mormon faith teaches, then logically it follows that children are said to be without sin, for they've not yet learned what sin is. But we know how to sin just fine before we know what it is because sin comes from within. Jesus said, "For out of the heart come evil thoughts, murder, adultery, sexual immorality, theft, false witness, slander" (Matthew 15:19). Doing these things is not what makes us sinful. We do them because we are sinful.

The law of God is a mirror that shows us our sin so that we may understand our need for a Savior (see also 1 Timothy 1:8-11 and James 1:22-25).

Note that D&C says, "little children are redeemed *from the foundation of the world* through mine Only Begotten." Who does the Bible say has been chosen for redemption from the foundation of the world through Jesus Christ? All Christians.

Ephesians 1:3-6 says, "Blessed be the God and Father of our Lord Jesus Christ, who has blessed us in Christ with every spiritual blessing in the heavenly places, even as he chose us in him before the foundation of the world, that we should be holy and blameless before him. In love he predestined us for adoption to himself as sons through Jesus Christ, according to the purpose of his will, to the praise of his glorious grace, with which he has blessed us in the Beloved."

3) The free agency of man is an eternal principle.

In the Book of Mormon, 2 Nephi 2:27 reads, "Wherefore, men are free according to the flesh; and all things are given them which are expedient unto man. And they are free to choose liberty and eternal life, through the great Mediator of all men, or to choose captivity and death, according to the captivity and power of the devil; for he seeketh that all men might be miserable like unto himself."

According to *Gospel Principles*, "God has told us through His prophets that we are free to choose between good and evil. We may choose liberty and eternal life by following Jesus Christ. We are also free to choose captivity and death by following Satan. The right to choose between good and evil and to act for ourselves is called agency."

One of the headlines says, "Agency Requires There Must Be a Choice." It says, "We cannot choose righteousness unless the opposites of good and evil are placed before us. Lehi, a great Book of Mormon prophet, told his son Jacob that in order to bring about the eternal purposes of God, there must be 'an opposition in all things. If not so… righteousness could not be brought to pass, neither wickedness, neither holiness nor misery, neither good nor bad' (2 Nephi 2:11)."[85]

What the Bible Says:

Titus 3:3-5 says, "For we ourselves were once foolish, disobedient, led astray, slaves to various passions and pleasures, passing our days in malice and envy, hated by others and hating one another.

---

[85] Chapter 4: Freedom to Choose, pg. 17-21.

But when the goodness and loving kindness of God our Savior appeared, he saved us, not because of works done by us in righteousness, but according to his own mercy."

Galatians 4:3-7 says that we "were enslaved to the elementary principles of the world. But when the fullness of time had come, God sent forth his Son, born of woman, born under the law, to redeem those who were under the law, so that we might receive adoption as sons. And because you are sons, God has sent the Spirit of his Son into our hearts, crying, 'Abba! Father!' So you are no longer a slave, but a son, and if a son, then an heir through God."

Before Christ sets us free, we're slaves to our sin. Everything we do is sin, for if it is not done to the glory of God, it is done to the glory of the self. Romans 14:23 says that whatever is not done in faith is sin. Isaiah 64:6 says that we are all unclean and even our best deeds are as a polluted garment before the Lord. It is Christ who washes us and makes us clean so that our deeds are acceptable to a holy God. It is Christ who frees us to be able to obey God in a right way.

A person can practice volition, but they cannot practice holy volition. You are given choices, but you can only choose what is in your nature to choose. It's not until God changes your nature and gives you his spirit that you're able to please him. You cannot please God unless his spirit dwells in you (Romans

8:8-9). The Bible says, "No one does good" (Romans 3:10). So how can you choose to please God, which would be a good thing?

Jesus said, "This is the work of God, that you believe in him whom he has sent. No one can come to me unless it is granted him by the Father" (John 6:29, 65). The reason why you are able to believe in Christ is because you are given belief. God freed you of your enslaved will and made you to believe according to his will.

The Mormon doctrine of free agency would call this a lie of Satan. In Mormon lore, this is exactly what Satan wanted to do—he wanted to make people believe against their will (Moses 4:1). In truth, it is God who works against our will to bring us to belief. We are incapable of believing in God any other way. Praise the Lord that he breaks the chains of bondage and sets us free!

4) A person can't eat or drink certain foods or they will break the Lord's law of health.

Doctrine and Covenants 89 gives very specific rules about what can and can't be consumed. According to *Gospel Principles*, "The Lord commands us not to use wine and strong drinks, meaning drinks containing alcohol. The First Presidency has taught that strong drink often brings cruelty, poverty, disease, and plague into the home. It often is a cause of dishonesty, loss of chastity, and loss of good judgment. It is a curse to all who drink it" (pg. 167-172).

It is also forbidden to drink hot drinks including tea and coffee, it is forbidden to use tobacco, and a person should try to stay away from anything that is habit-forming. Says *Gospel Principles*, "We purify our bodies so the Spirit of the Lord can dwell with us."

Doctrine and Covenants 89:18-19 says, "And all saints who remember to keep and do these sayings, walking in obedience to the commandments, shall receive health in their navel and marrow to their bones; And shall find wisdom and great treasures of knowledge, even hidden treasures."

What the Bible Says:

In Mark 7:15, Jesus said, "There is nothing outside a person that by going into him can defile him, but the things that come out of a person are what defile him." He went on to say, "Are you also without understanding? Do you not see that whatever goes into a person from outside cannot defile him, since it enters not his heart but his stomach, and is expelled?" Then verse 19 says, "Thus he declared all foods clean."

In 1 Timothy 4:1-5, we read the following: "Now the Spirit expressly says that in later times some will depart from the faith by devoting themselves to deceitful spirits and teachings of demons, through the insincerity of liars whose consciences are seared, who forbid marriage and require abstinence from foods that God created to be received with thanksgiving by those who believe and know the truth. For everything created by God is good, and nothing is to be rejected if it is received with thanksgiving, for it is made holy by the word of God and prayer."

The Bible definitely speaks against getting drunk (see Ephesians 5:18 and 1 Timothy 3:3) but in no way forbids any and all consumption of alcoholic drinks. On the contrary, the Apostle Paul told Timothy not to feel guilty about drinking wine (1 Timothy 5:23), and surely you know the story of Jesus changing the water to wine at the wedding in Cana (John 2:1-11).

Wine is referred to in the Scriptures as a symbol of God's great and abundant provision. In Proverbs 3:10, we read, "Your barns will be filled with plenty, and your vats will be bursting with wine." Psalm 104:15 speaks of "wine to gladden the heart of man, oil to make his face shine, and bread to strengthen man's heart."

Even the Lord's miracle at Cana was symbolic. The wedding had run out of wine, just as Israel had lost their zealous fervor for the Lord and were no longer receiving God's abundant blessing. They had grown stagnant and stale—obedient to the law of God, but their hearts were far from him.

Jesus came to give life and to give it more abundantly than ever before (see again John 10:10). He changed their stale water into wine—the best wine!

The master of the feast said, "Everyone serves the good wine first, and when people have drunk freely, then the poor wine. But you have kept the good wine until now" (John 2:10).

Though God had given Israel the law, it was not meant to save them, but to point to something better—his Son, Jesus Christ. All of the Law and the Prophets point to Christ. The miracle of changing water into wine happened at a wedding. Remember that the church, founded by Christ, is his bride.

We don't purify our bodies so the Spirit of the Lord can dwell with us. On the contrary, the Spirit of the Lord already dwells in all of those who are Christ's. It is for that reason we take care of our bodies. Again, not so the Spirit *will* dwell within us, but because he *does* (see 1 Corinthians 3:16, 6:19).

Also, we don't obey the laws of God to gain health and wealth. That's idolatry. Do not believe to receive something in return or you are elevating the gifts above the giver. Our desire for God must be greater than our desire comfortable living. People get sick and die not because they didn't believe right but because we live in a fallen world. Through our limitations and struggles, we are to be reminded that God's grace is sufficient for us, for his strength is made perfect in our weakness (2 Corinthians 12:9).

We should indeed enjoy the great things God has given us, including wine. Let it roll up into praise to our God! But like wine or beer or sex or food or entertainment or anything else God has given us to enjoy, we should partake in moderation and within the intended purpose God meant for such things to be enjoyed. Even good food can be gorged upon in a way that is self-destructive and irresponsible. But don't let anyone tell you that the partaking of these things is in and of itself a sin (see also Romans 14).

The Apostle Paul said to the Colossians, "Therefore let no one pass judgment on you in questions of food and drink, or with regard to a festival or a new moon or a Sabbath. These are a shadow of the things to come, but the substance belongs to Christ" (Colossians 2:16-17).

5) Paying tithes and offerings is a law that must be obeyed.

In Doctrine and Covenants 119:1-4, Joseph Smith prayed and asked God to show how much he required of his people for a tithe. The Lord answered, "This shall be the beginning of the tithing of my people. And after that, those who have thus been tithed shall pay one-tenth of all their interest annually; and this shall be a standing law unto them forever."[86]

According to *Gospel Principles*, "Anciently, Abraham and Jacob obeyed the commandment to pay a tithe of one-tenth of their increase (see Hebrews 7:1-

---

[86] According to the First Presidency, "interest" here is in reference to income.

10; Genesis 14:19-20; 28:20-22)" (pg. 184-188).

What the Bible Says:

There is no law requiring a tithe. The fact that *Gospel Principles* would reference Abraham and Jacob as having "obeyed the commandment" is funny because neither Abraham nor Jacob were commanded to tithe. They gave to the Lord willingly.

The tithe was first a pagan practice. A person who conquered or came into much wealth would give a tenth of what they acquired to the god or king of their choice. After Abraham (whose name was Abram at the time) rescued Lot and claimed the spoils of his enemies, he didn't want to give a tribute to any pagan king or that king would say, "I have made Abram rich." So he gave a tenth of his spoils to Melchizedek, king of Salem and priest of God Most High (see Genesis 14:17-24).

Abraham's act (and also Jacob's in Genesis 28:22) served as the basis for the tithe in Israel who were commanded to pay a tenth under the theocracy in which they lived. And there was more than one tithe—there was the Levitical tithe (Numbers 18:21, 24), the annual festival tithe (Deuteronomy 14:22-27), and the welfare tithe to the poor given every three years (Deuteronomy 14:28-29). The Levite priests, who received the Levitical tithe, were also supposed to tithe (Numbers 18:28).

Overall, the Israelites paid more like 23% in

tithes. Not included in that percentage was their free-will giving (Leviticus 23:38, Deuteronomy 15:10, 16:10). The tithe in Israel was actually a tax. What we draw from their example of tithing is not that we should give a tenth to the church, but rather that we should pay our taxes (see Matthew 17:24-27, Romans 13:7).

Now, don't misunderstand what I say—one should give to the church. The church cannot pay its bills, nor can the needs of the staff be met without such contributions. But it is not a fixed amount, and one will not be cursed if they don't meet that number (despite the insistence by many misguided preachers that Malachi 3:8-9 means a person who doesn't tithe will be under a curse).

Paul said in 1 Corinthians 16:1-2, "Now concerning the collection for the saints: as I directed the churches of Galatia, so you also are to do. On the first day of every week, each of you is to put something aside and store it up, as he may prosper, so that there will be no collecting when I come." That last part is to indicate that giving should be a regular thing, not just when a specific need arises. And notice that Paul never mentions an amount.

Paul also told the Corinthians that their gift was to be willing and ready, "not as an exaction. The point is this: whoever sows sparingly will also reap sparingly, and whoever sows bountifully will also reap bountifully. Each must give as he has decided in his heart, not reluctantly or under compulsion, for God loves a cheerful giver" (2 Corinthians 9:5-7). Jesus said your giving should "be in secret. And your Father who sees in secret will reward you."

A person should give what they can give, and that is between them and the Lord. If they can give a lot, and they desire in their hearts to give a lot, then they should give a lot. But a person who can't give as much should not feel ashamed. No church should bully its congregants into believing they must give a certain percentage, or else.

If you don't know how much to give to the church, pray that the Lord will show you how much to give. If anyone lacks wisdom, he should ask of God (James 1:5).

It is through these kinds of laws—like what a person can eat or drink or how much they should tithe—that the Mormon church places a legalistic burden on its congregants they cannot bear. This is exactly what the Pharisees did—made up laws that people had to follow in order to earn their salvation. No one can earn salvation. God saves us by his grace. If you had to work to achieve it, then it would not be grace.

Galatians 5:1 says, "For freedom Christ has set us free; stand firm therefore, and do not submit again to a yoke of slavery." Jesus said, "Come to me, all who labor and are heavy laden, and I will give you rest. Take my yoke upon you, and learn from me, for I am gentle and lowly in heart, and you will find rest for your souls. For my yoke is easy, and my burden is light" (Matthew 11:28-30).

6) Light skin is a sign of blessing, and dark skin is a sign of a curse.

In the Book of Mormon, 2 Nephi 5:21 reads, "And he had caused the cursing to come upon them, yea, even a sore cursing, because of their iniquity. For behold, they had hardened their hearts against him, that they had become like unto a flint; wherefore, as they were white, and exceedingly fair and delightsome, that they might not be enticing unto my people the Lord God did cause a skin of blackness to come upon them."

Alma 3:6 says, "And the skins of the Lamanites were dark, according to the mark which was set upon their fathers, which was a curse upon them because of their transgression and their rebellion against their brethren." In 3 Nephi 2:15-16, it says, "And their curse was taken from them, and their skin became white like unto the Nephites; And their young men and their daughters became exceedingly fair."

In the Pearl of Great Price, Moses 7:8 says, "For behold, the Lord shall curse the land with much heat, and the barrenness thereof shall go forth forever; and there was a blackness came upon all the children of Canaan, that they were despised among all people." Verse 22 says, "And Enoch also beheld the residue of the people which were the sons of Adam; and they were a mixture of all the seed of Adam save it was the seed of Cain, for the seed of Cain were black, and had not place among them."

Brigham Young said, "Why are so many of the inhabitants of the earth cursed with a skin of blackness? It comes in consequence of their fathers rejecting the power of the holy priesthood, and the law of God. They will go down to death. And when all the rest of the children have received their blessings in the holy priesthood, then that curse will be removed from the seed of Cain, and they will then come up and possess the priesthood, and receive all the blessings which we are now entitled to."

This comment of Young's was recalled in *A Statement by the First Presidency* made on August 17, 1949. They said, "The attitude of the Church with reference to Negroes remains as it has always stood. It is not a matter of the declaration of a policy but of direct commandment from the Lord." They said, "Negroes may become members of the Church, but that they are not entitled to the priesthood at the present time."

This ban ended in 1978 when President Spencer W. Kimball and other LDS leaders claimed to have received a revelation from the Lord permitting them to extend all the privileges of the church to every worthy member, regardless of race or color.[87]

---

[87] Church News, Vol. 48, No. 24. June 17, 1978.

However, Brigham Young had said that should the day come when blacks are allowed to become partakers in the priesthood, "On that very day, and hour we should do so, the priesthood is taken from this church and the kingdom of God leaves us to our fate. The moment we consent to mingle with the seed of Cain, the Church must go to destruction."[88]

Joseph Smith advocated for slave owners to be kind to their slaves. But he said that it was no business of anyone's to tell the southern states that owning slaves was wrong, since the Negro slaves were the cursed sons of Ham.[89]

This is something the religion would rather sweep under the rug. But their history of prejudice against blacks is abundant, and the documentation is plentiful. No matter how receptive Mormonism is of blacks now, their most sacred scriptures still favor white people and repudiate black people. To this day, the black population in the state of Utah is well below the national average (1% of Utah is black, 12% nationwide).

What the Bible Says:

In Matthew 28:19-20, Jesus said, "Go therefore and make disciples of all nations, baptizing them in

---

[88] The Complete Discourses of Brigham Young, vol. 1, January 5, 1852, pg. 470-471.

[89] The Joseph Smith Papers, Letter to Oliver Cowdery, April 9, 1836.

the name of the Father and of the Son and of the Holy Spirit, teaching them to observe all that I have commanded you. And behold, I am with you always, to the end of the age."

In Acts 10:34-35, Peter said, "Truly I understand that God shows no partiality, but in every nation anyone who fears him and does what is right is acceptable to him."

In Acts 17:26-27, Paul said, "And he made from one man every nation of mankind to live on all the face of the earth, having determined allotted periods and the boundaries of their dwelling place, that they should seek God, and perhaps feel their way toward him and find him. Yet he is actually not far from each one of us."

Romans 10:11-13 reads, "For the Scripture says, 'Everyone who believes in him will not be put to shame.' For there is no distinction between Jew and Greek; for the same Lord is Lord of all, bestowing his riches on all who call on him. For 'everyone who calls on the name of the Lord will be saved.'"

Colossians 3:11 says, "Here there is not Greek and Jew, circumcised and uncircumcised, barbarian, Scythian, slave, free; but Christ is all, and in all."

The Apostle John described this vision of heaven: "After this I looked, and behold, a great multitude that no one could number, from every nation, from all tribes and peoples and languages, standing before the throne and before the Lamb, clothed in white robes, with palm branches in their hands, and crying out with a loud voice, 'Salvation belongs to our God who sits on the throne, and to the Lamb!'" (Revelation 7:9-10).

Joseph Smith simply did not understand the mark of Cain—it was not a curse, but God's mercy! After Cain had killed his brother Abel and God exiled him to wander the earth, Cain said, "My punishment is greater than I can bear. Behold, you have driven me today away from the ground, and from your face I shall be hidden. I shall be a fugitive and a wanderer on the earth, and whoever finds me will kill me."

The Lord said to him, "Not so! If anyone kills Cain, vengeance shall be taken on him sevenfold." Genesis 4:15 says, "And the Lord put a mark on Cain, lest any who found him should attack him."

The mark was not to show that he was cursed. It was to show that he was protected, and anyone that harmed him would themselves be cursed. No where does it say that mark was black skin. The shade of a person's skin is simply the amount of melanin a they have. It does make one person better than another.

7) Plural marriage is part of the new and everlasting covenant.

Mormonism is a plural-marriage religion, an issue that the church has gone back and forth over. In 1830, Joseph Smith said that a man shall have one wife. According to the Book of Mormon, Jacob 2:27 reads, "Wherefore, my brethren, hear me, and harken to the word of the Lord: For there shall not any man among you have save it be one wife; and concubines he shall have none."

However, in 1843, Joseph Smith received a new revelation from the Lord related to the new and everlasting covenant that included the principle of plural marriage. Smith inquired of God why Abraham, Isaac, Jacob, Moses, David, and Solomon had many wives and concubines. God's response is in Doctrine and Covenants 132.

Verse 4 states, "For behold, I reveal unto you a new and everlasting covenant; and if ye abide not that covenant, then are ye damned; for no one can reject this covenant and be permitted to enter into my glory."

Verses 34 says, "God commanded Abraham, and Sarah gave Hagar to Abraham to wife. And why did she do it? Because this was the law; and from Hagar sprang many people. This, therefore, was fulfilling, among other things, the promises." Verse 37 continues, "Abraham received concubines, and they bore him children; and it was accounted unto him for righteousness," and also says that Isaac and Jacob "are gods." Verse 38 says that David, Solomon, and Moses also received many wives and concubines given to them by God and did not sin.

Verses 61-62 say, "If any man espouse a virgin,

and desire to espouse another, and the first give her consent, and if he espouse the second, and they are virgins, and have vowed to no other man, then he is justified; he cannot commit adultery for they are given unto him; for he cannot commit adultery with they that belongeth unto him and to no one else. And if he have ten virgins given unto him by this law, he cannot commit adultery, for they belong to him, and they are given unto him; therefore is he justified."

The practice of plural marriage came to an end in 1890 by LDS President Wilford Woodruff who said he received a revelation from God. This was only after the U.S. government passed laws to make the practice illegal, and the U.S. Supreme Court upheld them.[90]

In 1998, Former Mormon President Gordon B. Hinckley said the following: "This Church has nothing whatever to do with those practicing polygamy. They are not members of this Church... If any of our members are found to be practicing plural marriage, they are excommunicated, the most serious penalty the Church can impose. Not only are those so involved in direct violation of the civil law, they are in violation of the law of this Church."

The Book of Mormon prohibits polygamy, but Doctrine and Covenants promotes it. According to

---

[90] See Doctrine and Covenants, Official Declaration 1. Remember, one of the things Joseph Smith was imprisoned for at the end of his life was polygamy.

the new and everlasting covenant given by God to Joseph Smith, plural marriage cannot be abolished or it's not an *everlasting* covenant. For the time being, it's only on hiatus.

What the Bible Says:

In Matthew 19:4-8, Jesus said, "Have you not read that he who created them from the beginning made them male and female, and said, 'Therefore a man shall leave his father and his mother and hold fast to his wife, and the two shall become one flesh'? So they are no longer two but one flesh. What therefore God has joined together let man not separate."

The Pharisees said, "Why then did Moses command one to give a certificate of divorce and to send her away?" Jesus replied, "Because your hearts were hard, Moses allowed you to divorce your wives, but from the beginning it was not so."

Even though there are instances where men like Abraham, Jacob, David, and Solomon had multiple wives, this was not the way marriage was intended to be. From the very beginning, God designed marriage to be between one man and one woman for life. Polygamy is never blessed nor encouraged by God anywhere in the Bible. Perhaps God allowed it, as Moses allowed divorce, but it's not his intention for marriage.

Speaking of Moses, he didn't have multiple wives—he only had one. In Exodus 2:21, he married a Midianite woman named Zipporah. In Numbers 12:1, it says that Aaron and Miriam, Moses' brother and sister, conflicted with him "because of the Cushite woman whom he had married." Some have theorized that this suggests another wife, but it's still the same woman. According to Habakkuk 3:7, Cush and Midian are the same place. Likewise, Isaac didn't have multiple wives. The only wife ever mentioned is Rebekah.

Deuteronomy 17:17 says, "He shall not acquire many wives for himself, lest his heart turn away, nor shall he acquire for himself excessive silver and gold." This is precisely what happened to both David and Solomon. They had many wives and many treasures, and their hearts turned from God (Solomon more-so than his father, David, as David notably repented).

Joseph Smith's claim that Sarah gave Hagar to Abraham as a wife according to the law of God is dumb-founding. It is another evidence that Smith simply did not know the Scriptures. God promised Abraham that he would make him the father of many nations. However, Sarah was beyond child-bearing years and "the way of women had ceased to be with her" (Genesis 18:11). So she gave her maid-servant, Hagar, to Abraham to sleep with her and bear him a son (he did not marry Hagar).

Hagar had a son named Ishmael, but Abraham and Sarah were trying to initiate God's promise on their own. Ishmael was not the heir God promised. In fact, God told Hagar that Ishmael's descendants would rise up against his kinsmen (Genesis 16:11-12). Eventually, God told Abraham to send Ishmael away (Genesis 21:12). The promised seed was Isaac, born of Sarah, Abraham's wife.

Romans 9:7-8 says, "Not all are children of Abraham because they are his offspring, but 'Through Isaac shall your offspring be named.' This means that it is not the children of the flesh who are the children of God, but the children of the promise are counted as offspring." Ishmael and his descendants are not part of the promise.

Among the qualifications of a pastor or an elder in the church listed in 1 Timothy 3:1-7 and Titus 1:5-9, it says in both places that he must be "the husband of one wife." He is to be an example for the rest of the church.

Just as the Mormon scriptures teach that there are many gods, so their scriptures teach that a man can have many wives. But the God of the Bible is only one God, and Christ our only Savior has only one bride, the church. So should every man who is married be united to only one wife.

8) The restored gospel must be preached to every nation and people.

In the Mormon scriptures, preaching the gospel began with Adam: "And thus the Gospel began to be preached, from the beginning" (Moses 5:58). It continued with Joseph Smith: "And this gospel shall be preached unto every nation, and kindred, and tongue, and people" (from Doctrine and Covenants 133:37).

According to the Mormon publication *True to the Faith*, "The Lord has declared that missionary work is a responsibility of all Latter-day Saints (see D&C 88:81)... The most powerful missionary message that you can send is your own example of living a happy Latter-day Saint life" (2004, pg. 105).

Missionary work includes helping and supporting those who join the Church, going door-to-door in one's own community, and going to another country to do missions abroad. Missions work in our mortal, earthly existence prepares us for missions work in the life to come, as Mormons will be traveling from paradise to the spirit prison to witness to the non-Mormons incarcerated there.

What the Bible Says:

Jesus is the gospel (Mark 1:1), and only the true Jesus of the Bible is the true gospel.

As has been demonstrated in previous chapters, Joseph Smith often displayed a poor understanding of words. The word gospel means "good news." It wasn't used until Jesus came because he is the good news. There is no Old Testament equivalent of the word. The Apostle Paul said in Ephesians 3:1-6 that this gospel was a mystery to those prior to Christ's coming, and it has only since been revealed through his apostles.

The "gospel" that the Mormons preach is a false gospel. It originates from a man who was a liar and a con-artist, who twisted the Scriptures and weaved many false tales, who manipulated thousands of people—and to this day, millions of people—who married many women and stole the wives of other men, who continually broke the law and reaped what he sowed.

The God of the Mormon faith is a false god, one god among many gods, an exalted man who sinned and had to complete a process of becoming divine. The Mormon Jesus is a different Jesus than the Christ of the Bible. He is literally Satan's brother, who has a beginning and is not the creator of all things, and whose blood does not atone for all sin.

The Mormon way of salvation is not by the sufficient grace of God but by the works of man. The Mormon faith is a different gospel. It cannot save.

Once again from Galatians 1:6-9, "I am astonished that you are so quickly deserting him who called you in the grace of Christ and are turning to a different gospel—not that there is another one, but there are some who trouble you and want to distort the gospel of Christ. But even if we or an angel from heaven should preach to you a gospel contrary to the one we preached to you, let him be accursed. As we have said before, so now I say again: If anyone is preaching to you a gospel contrary to the one you received, let him be accursed."

John 3:36 says, "Whoever believes in the Son has eternal life; whoever does not obey the Son shall not see life, but the wrath of God remains on him." We do not have forgiveness of sins and right-standing with God any other way or through any other Jesus—only the true Jesus of the true word of God. The Bible says to speak the truth in love (Ephesians 4:15). If the message is not true, it is not loving.

We ourselves should heed the command to go out with the true gospel and make disciples of all nations, as Christ had commissioned his disciples to do, teaching all that he had commanded, baptizing in the name of the Father and of the Son and of the Holy Spirit (Matthew 28:18-20). We must teach the sound words of Christ and rebuke those who contradict it (Titus 1:9), but we must do this with gentleness and respect (1 Peter 3:15).

The Bible says, "The Lord's servant must not be quarrelsome but kind to everyone, able to teach, patiently enduring evil, correcting his opponents with gentleness. God may perhaps grant them repentance leading to a knowledge of the truth, and they may come to their senses and escape from the snare of the devil, after being captured by him to do his will" (2 Timothy 2:24-26).

If you are a Christian witnessing to a Mormon, you must speak the truth in love, with gentleness and respect. They have been ensnared by Satan, as we all once were before we were set free by the hearing of the gospel.

If you are a Mormon reading this book, I implore you to leave the lies you have been told and cling to the truth of the gospel of Jesus Christ—according to what the Bible says, not according to what Joseph Smith said. It will not be easy for you. Your family may hate you. Your friends will ostracize you and turn their backs on you. It's the way the Mormon religion was built. But it is in love that I say this to you, and it is in love that I have written this book.

Psalm 27:10 says, "For my father and my mother have forsaken me, but the Lord will take me in." Jesus said, "Blessed are you when others revile you and persecute you and utter all kinds of evil against you falsely on my account. Rejoice and be glad, for your reward is great in heaven, for so they persecuted the prophets before you" (Matthew 5:11-12).

Only by faith in the true gospel will you be saved from death and the judgment of God. You will be adopted into his family as his son or daughter, sealed for the day of redemption by his Holy Spirit, safe in his love through his Son, Jesus Christ.

Romans 1:16 says, "I am not ashamed of the gospel, for it is the power of God for salvation to everyone who believes."

27747192R00083

Made in the USA
Lexington, KY
08 January 2019